Dreadnought
Slim Jim
FLIPPER
Catchumbig
Luny Frog
WEE DEE
FLATFISH
Live-Wire
BITE EM
Chautauqua
Spindiver
PIKIE
Getsem
Dummy-Double
EXPERT
CHAMPION
Water Scout
GLOBE
Roamer
REVOLUTION
ECLIPSE
Roman Spider
Chippewa
Hungry Jack
Coaxer
Gar
O'BOY
VAMP
Stump Dodger
SLOPENOSE
Floater
Jigger
Nifty Minne
BASS CALLER
Crawdad
Panatella
Charmer
MAYBUG
Tantalizer
Tadpolly
Gloworm
KINNEY BIRD
PIKIE
HUMDINGER
Sarasota
PAL-O-MINE
KILLER
SHAKER
Bassy Getum
Ladybug Wiggler
PLOPPER
Little Wonder
Gamefisher
HOOKZUM
Tango
HELL DIVER
SPOOK
Evolution
Hydroplane
Punkinseed
RIVER RUNT
River Rustler
Jazz Wiggler
T.N.T.
Redfin
WAGTAIL
MERMAID
Zig-Zag
Water Witch
Tom Thumb
Flying Helgramite
Castrola
Woodpecker
BASS ORENO
S.O.S.
Flip-Flop
BASSER
FISH NIPPLE
Dingbat
SNAKERBAIT
The Ghost
Crazy Crawler
Vacuum Bait
Safe Deposit Bait
Bass Hog
SURPRISE
Struggling Mouse
LUCKY 13
Panatella
SPOONJACK
WHIRLWIND
Rotary Marvel
Crab Wiggler
Truck-Oreno
VAMP
WOW
Croaker
Teaser
SCOOP
DINGBAT
Bassmerizer
Pearl Plug
999
TORPEDO
Tin' Liz
Pull Me Slow
Artistic
WEEDLESS WIDOW
Bass Seeker
Plunker
KINNEY BIRD
BEETLE
BOMBER
CYCLONE
FLAPTAIL
BLACK SUCKER
Wiggle King

A collection of vintage fishing tackle catalogs and brochures.

THE LIFE AND LEGEND OF SHERIDAN R. JONES:

AMERICA'S PIONEERING OUTDOOR WRITER AND HIS SEARCH

FOR THE PERFECT FISHING LURE

JOSEPH HILKO

Good Luck Fishin"

Joe Hilko

The Whitefish Press
WWW.WHITEFISHPRESS.COM
WHITEFISHPRESS@YAHOO.COM

8/21/2017

The Whitefish Press is an imprint of Micropress America, L.L.C.

ISBN 10: 0-9815102-8-0
ISBN 13: 978-0-9815102-8-6

Table of Contents

Acknowledgments

It was the fishing expeditions to remote ponds and lakes in the 1950s that sparked an excitement in a 12-year old boy that would last a lifetime. These trips were under the cover of moonlight when even the most wary of largemouth bass would fall prey to any movement of an artificial lure that resembled a frog, mouse, or small fish on the waters surface. Thank you Uncles John, Charles, and Peter Sarnecky and Uncle George Hilko for all the memories and a lifetime of passion for the sport of fishing. Thank you Scoutmaster Chet Looman and Explorer advisor Karl Petraske for the many adventure camping, fishing, and canoeing in the remote Adirondack New York trout ponds, the Fulton Chain lakes and Raquette river, and the Canadian wilderness of Algonquin National Park and North Bay, Ontario. Also, special thanks to all my fishing and camping partners. including John Borkowski, David Petraske, Theodore Retajczyk, my wife Lynne, my Dad Joe Sr., and brother Philip, and others who were always there to share the fun moments and fishing accomplishments as well as the sad disappointments when the big one would sometimes get away. Happy and eventful fishing trips to all wherever you are.

Also, you know you're hooked on the challenges of bass fishing when you must awake at 4:00 AM to get an early start on the day. Your best chance for success is just when the morning fog is lifting from the still lake water and your cast is accurate as your artificial lure selection arrives at the edge of a lily pad. It's the science in fishing that motivates the interest in all the unique lure offerings possible that will increase this chance for success. The National Fishing Lure Collectors Club, P. O. Box 509, Mansfield, Texas, 76063 - provided the vehicle to buy, trade, or sell almost any artificial lure imaginable either new or old. It was a fellow NFLCC member John Affolter of Oregon City, Oregon who found the cache of Sheridan R. Jones personal tackle and lure collection and made its purchase possible. Consequently, the historical nature of the Sheridan R. Jones collection was worthy of special documentation in a book which resulted in the compiling of the multitude of Sheridan's writings and a visit to Iowa Falls for research on the life of Professor Jones and the people who knew him. Thank you immensely to all the people of Ellsworth College and Iowa Falls, Iowa: Duane Lloyd in the Dean's Office; Bill Schmidt; Rich A Wheeler; Dorothy Chaplin; Mike Fisher; Bob and Debbie Anders; and the Iowa Falls Rotary Club for their hospitality.

Finally, this Sheridan R. Jones book would not have been possible if not for the helpful assistance of photographer David Felano of Burnt Hills, New York and the organization of the wealth of Sheridan's documents by Eileen Parzek, Albany, New York, and Dr. Todd Larson, Cincinnati, Ohio.

-- Joseph Hilko
Ballston Spa, New York

A pair of classic fishing tackle ads from Outer's Book, when Sheridan Jones was the magazine's editor.

Period ads showing a few of Jones' favorite tackle companies.

Chapter 1:

THE MYSTERY OF SHERIDAN JONES

I n his 1952 edition of *Black Bass Fishing*, noted outdoor writer Robert Page Lincoln wrote that Sheridan R. Jones was "the man who disappeared." At one time a prominent angling author, editor of *Outdoor Recreation*, keen bass angler, and author of *Black Bass and Bass Craft*, Sheridan Jones became the most overlooked writer in the American angling field.

It appears that what happened to Sheridan Ross Jones also happened to thousands of other Americans in the 1930s during the Great Depression. As Dean and Biology Professor of Ellsworth College in Iowa Falls, Iowa, he had to turn all of his efforts toward saving the educational institution from extinction. In Iowa Falls, the depression hit particularly hard as grain prices were in

Bob Lincoln, in the heart of the lake country.

SHERIDAN R. JONES

S.R. Jones, often referred to as "Prof", came to Ellsworth as a young man and remained for a half century. He served the College in many capacities which are detailed throughout the written material. Several generations of graduates remember him as instructor, dean, and friend. [Source: Early copies of the WEB.]

rapid decline and jobs were hard to come by. Prior to the Great Depression, Sheridan Jones was one of the most prolific angling writers in this country for a period of sixteen years; however, in the end, Sheridan's dedication to his life's work, and the students of Ellsworth College, were a priority over all else.

The story of Sheridan Jones' outdoor writing career, his lifetime dedicated to education, and ultimately his impact on the community of Iowa Falls, Iowa, are at the heart of the story of Sheridan R. Jones—one of the most prominent writers of his era, and the man "who disappeared."

Sheridan Jones was Dean and Biology Professor at Ellsworth College.

During his eighteen years as an active outdoor writer, Sheridan wrote many articles for *Outer's Book and Recreation* and *Outdoor Recreation*, and was able to accumulate hundreds of fishing tackle items (lures, reels, rods, lines and tackle) given to him from both new and existing fishing tackle companies. He obviously couldn't fish or use all this tackle so he saved and collected these fishing items for the future as original examples of American made fishing tackle. In the following pages, you will see many of the lures and products he received directly from the various fishing tackle factories; today they are considered original classics in the truest sense of the word.

In addition to companies like South Bend, Sheridan Jones endorsed tackle from almost every major firm. This neat "Eat Oreno" piece—actually a Baby Bass Oreno lure in copper finish—was an invitation and favor for a South Bend sales banquet in 1926 involving dozens of the top men of industry and fishing in America, including Sheridan Jones, Notre Dame football coach Knute Rockne, The Sporting News publisher J.G. Taylor Spink, and G.M. and J.M. Studebaker, the famed carmakers. The name "Eat Oreno" was coined for this "lure favor," and used for this banquet only. It was not a catalog item.

The lures are preserved in the exact same packaging and condition as when first produced in the period from 1913-1929 and sent to Sheridan R. Jones for his review and stamp of approval.

This book also includes excerpts from many of the original angling articles written by Sheridan Jones, containing a wealth of information

The 1915 Baits--A Tackle Screed In Two Casts

By SHERIDAN R. JONES

WITH ILLUSTRATIONS FROM PHOTOGRAPHS BY THE AUTHOR

[Editors Note: This article appears in two parts. Some manufacturers were unable to get their baits to the author in time for the March issue. There will be others just as unique in the issue for April.]

about fish, eco-systems, fishing strategy, outdoor activities, and proper tackle and lures. These articles are primary source materials, useful for individual interpretation.

Sport fishing is the number one participation sport enjoyed by men, women and children of all ages. The fish lure makers have always been looking to make the most perfect lure to capitalize on this widespread popularity. The competition in lure making was intense, and there was an onslaught of hundreds of new lure companies originating in early twentieth century America, resulting in many trips to the patent office by the lure creators. Significant study and insight into the science of fishing also began at this time. New developments in fishing lures, rods, reels, tackle and techniques during that period are explored and discussed in the angling articles written by Sheridan R. Jones. These were widely circulated around the country in magazines, newspapers, pamphlets, booklets, and catalogs of the era. The following pages are full of the pictures of mostly original specimens of these first lures owned by Sheridan Jones. These lures were made by the emerging fishing tackle companies of that time.

It was the mass machine production of synthetic materials, such as plastic and rubber developed in the 1940s and 1950s, that eliminated and replaced the slow and expensive process of crafting handmade lures. We will never again see the artwork, designs, and crafted distinction these rare lures display. These heirlooms of the fishing world, representing the search for the perfect lure, are truly America's heritage, and Sheridan Jones played a significant role in not only promoting them, but informing anglers everywhere on which ones worked most effectively. As such, he was one of the most influential outdoor writers of the era, a man whose opinions were sought by informed readers across the nation and whose endorsement was widely coveted by tackle manufacturers of all stripes.

Sheridan Jones' very own tackle box full of his new Creek Chub lures. They are as follows: 1) Midget Pikie Minnow (painted eyes); 2) Crawdad; 3) Sarasota; 4) Pikie Minnow; 5) Plunker; 6) Baby Wiggle Fish; 7) Husky Musky; 8) Wiggle Fish; 9) Baby Injured Minnow; 10) Fintail Shiner; 11) Injured Minnow. Many of these lures were sold for five decades or more.

Moments in History / Places in Time

A. SHERIDAN JONES

S *heridan Jones' father, Augustus Sheridan Jones, was a pioneer and veteran of the American Civil War who moved to what was then called Dakota Territory in 1872. Up until 1870, the region was very sparsely populated but experienced a major growth spurt beginning that year known as the "Dakota Boom" that continued throughout the 1870s. When A.S. Jones set up his homestead he also founded the town of Olivet. The town soon grew and he became both a penmanship teacher and eventually, after studying law, the District Attorney of nearby Hutchinson. More on A.S. Jones' life is covered in the next chapter.*

Like his son, he was also believed in the importance of education, and was responsible for a several hundred page hand written report recommending that the Dakota Territorial Governor adopt both a Township system of schools and a Territorial Board of Education to oversee it. This was a progressive educational idea for the time and necessary if the Territory wanted to be considered for statehood, and it served to greatly influence education in the region during the Territorial era (1869-1889). On November 2, 1889, Dakota Territory was formally admitted into the Union as the states of North and South Dakota.

A. SHERIDAN JONES

Life was difficult in the Dakotas. Periodic drought troubled farmers and occasional conflict with Native Americans erupted into the Sioux Wars of 1890-91. The Sioux Wars ended tragically with the death of the great Sioux leader Sitting Bull in 1890, followed soon after by the Massacre at Wounded Knee when up to 350 Sioux men, women, and children were killed by U.S. Cavalry.

A. Sheridan Jones died in 1893 from tuberculosis, called at the time consumption. Tuberculosis was a common and often fatal infectious disease for which there was no known cure at the time.

Chapter 2:

EARLY LIFE

Sheridan Ross Jones was born to a pioneer family on August 23, 1881. His father was Augustus Sheridan Jones, of Welsh and Yankee extraction. Augustus served in the Third Wisconsin Infantry during the Civil War and was wounded at the famed battles of Antietam and Gettysburg. Sheridan's mother, Mary Barbara Ross Jones, immigrated to the United States at the age of 12 and

A sod hut on the Dakota Prairie ca. 1875.

came from the adventurous German Ross family. She spoke German and Russian, and raised Sheridan and his two sisters, teaching them the simple pleasures of pioneer living. It is from these humble beginnings that Sheridan R. Jones developed a love of the land and its creatures, as well as the practical use of firearms and fishing rods.

Moving westward through Wisconsin, the Jones family settled in the Dakota Territory. This was about the time that the Dakota Territory was transitioning from sod huts to frame houses. Sheridan's father established an early pioneer newspaper in 1869 at Memmo called *The Rural Voice*. He traveled daily between Memmo and his home at Olivet, Dakota by horse and buggy with

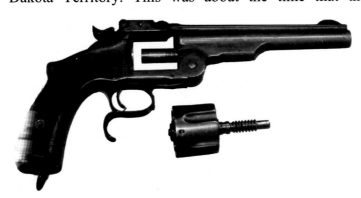

Guns like this Smith & Wesson .38 pistol were necessary tools of life on the Dakota frontier.

his trusted Smith and Wesson .38 Caliber Revolver. Gun toting was a necessary part of life in the days of the rugged frontier, especially for a newspaperman with an editorial column! His gun was later kept and cherished by his son Sheridan throughout his life. Augustus Jones also served on the Dakota Territorial Legislature, which helped carve the Dakotas into states. He later became the first Superintendent of Public Instruction and aided in the establishment of South Dakota State University at Vermillion. Besides being a newspaper editor, Sheridan's father was also a lawyer, professor and poet, but sadly, died very young from tuberculosis. Sheridan's mother lived to a ripe old age of 94, which was astounding in those days.

In 1893, at the age of 12, Sheridan entered the Preparatory Department of the University of South Dakota. It was at this young age that he became interested in fishing and hunting. He liked shooting and hunting but didn't have the best equipment, so, while working at a local hardware store, he decided it was time for a new shotgun. He conceived the idea of selling chances to win his old one, and ended up selling all of the chances except one. Urged to buy the last chance himself, he did, and as luck would have it, won back his own shotgun. He had also made enough money to buy a brand new Winchester 1897. Sheridan would spend many early mornings while attending school with his pals shooting ducks and geese on the Missouri River bottoms, and out on the prairie hunting grouse. Sheridan was so good that he became a member of the South Dakota Trap Team, which won the State Championship for a number of years. In the academics department Sheridan won honors for his debated speeches at the University. He decided not to following in his father's footsteps and become a lawyer and instead chose to pursue a career in the biological sciences, where he met Dr. Lewis Akely, brother of the well-known Carl E. Akely. Science classes were held in Akely's laboratory and Sheridan was introduced to the new world of the biological sciences. Sheridan's enthusiasm for the sciences was also motivated by his love of the outdoors and nature.

University of South Dakota's University Hall, ca. 1920, Vermillions, S.D.

DID YOU KNOW

The only way pioneer woodsmen like Sheridan could communicate with each other was by rifle fire!

The University of South Dakota did not have the necessary science laboratory with bird and animal exhibits for study, so during the summer months, Sheridan joined an expedition team following cattle trails in the uncharted parts of South Dakota. There were no railroads west of the Missouri River so travel was difficult, mainly undertaken on foot with supplies carried and stored in a chuck wagon. The turn of the century expedition collected specimens for the University science laboratory, and additionally made a geological and biological survey of the state.

The years of expeditions and surveying in the Dakotas allowed Sheridan to spend many hours at his favorite past times: hunting and fishing. Sheridan became the official "shooter" of the exhibition for food (game) and honed his fishing expertise in the abundant rivers, lakes and streams.

One of the specimens found for the University science lab was an albino rattlesnake. After he became a biology professor, it became a conversation piece in Sheridan's science classes for years. Gathering specimens over the years also allowed Sheridan to become an accomplished taxidermist. He collected many rare birds and animals that met with natural and accidental deaths and preserved these models for exhibits and instructional use in science classes. Many of those original mounted specimens of birds and wildlife from the Sheridan Jones collection are still seen and studied today at the Calkins Nature Center Museum in Iowa Falls, Iowa.

Sheridan Jones graduated from the University of South Dakota in 1902 and remained until 1906, completing a Master's of Science degree. According to a University of South Dakota yearbook, Sheridan was "a fellow who studies when the spirit moves him, but hunts and fishes the rest of the time." His work as a taxidermist helped pay his way

Mounted birds from the Jones collection, on display at Ellsworth College's Calkins Nature Center

through the University. In 1906, Sheridan took a teaching job at the Baptist College at Grand Island, Nebraska. One evening, Sheridan and a faculty friend decided to attend the theater where a road company, which was very popular in those days, was performing "Julius Caesar," the Shakespearian play. The next day, his teaching career almost ended when the Dean reprimanded both, as teachers were not supposed to attend theater.

That Christmas in 1906, Sheridan traveled back to Vermillion, South Dakota where the University was located and his family lived, and married his young sweetheart, Mae Freeman. It was in 1908 that Mr. and Mrs. Sheridan Jones moved to Iowa Falls, Iowa so he could become biology professor at Ellsworth College (see letter of appointment on the following page).

Ellsworth College, founded in 1890, was at the time going through a period of growth, and had just received nearly 5000 acres of land to use as an endowment. The hiring of Sheridan Jones was part of the college's plan to restructure the curriculum and better position itself in the competitive educational market. They didn't know it at the time, but the hiring of Sheridan R. Jones was one of the most important in the college's history.

An advertising card for Sheridan Jones' Ornamental Taxidermy; taxidermy was one of the most important ways to teach animal biology to young students, a tradition dating back to the time of Charles Darwin, also a taxidermist.

S. R. Jones Comes to Ellsworth

Ellsworth College
Iowa Falls, Iowa.

I. F. MEYER, PHI B., A. M.
PRESIDENT.

June 19, 1908.

Prof. Sheridan R. Jones,

Grand Island, Neb.

My dear Mr. Jones:--

I presented your application to our Board of Trustees at their meeting June the 16th. They would like to have you take up the work here and I am authorized to say that no maximum salary has yet been fixed for this chair. However, the board states that you may expect advancement if you accept the place and succeed in your work.

The College here is just getting thoroughly organized; our endowment coming to us only last year in the form of 4992 acres of good Iowa land. This is to be sold and the money invested in conservative investments. While at present we have some income from the land it is not large enough to warrant us in paying at the present time as large salaries as we hope to in the near future. Nevertheless, our successful men will be advanced some each year and there is opportunity here better than in any other of the small Colleges with which I am acquainted.

With reference to the questions you ask, I may say that your salary is absolutely safe to be paid in full. The salary does not include the summer school, being only for the regular thirty six weeks of the College year. The board have authorised me to state to you that they will pay you a salary of Nine Hundred Dollars ($900) for your first year of nine months and they are willing to say that you will have advancement yearly to the extent of their ability to grant it, providing you are successful in your work. Please let me have your early reply. I shall hope that you can see your way clear to join us.

I remain,

Very truly yours,

F. F. Meyer.

[Source: Bill Schmidt]

Sheridan Jones' appointment letter dated 19 June 1908. Note the annual salary of $900 (not including summer school), the equivalent of $20,920 in today's terms.

Moments in History / Places in Time

IOWA FALLS CA. 1910

Iowa Falls, the home of Ellsworth College, is a town in Hardin County, Iowa and is located on the beautiful Iowa River in the north central part of the state. Its nickname is "The Scenic City."

Founded in 1855 by J.L. Estis and Homer Stevens, Iowa Falls was known for decades as a hub for the local railroad lines. Beginning in 1866, the community was served by a number of railways, ranging from the Illinois Central to the Short Line Railway, originated by E.L. Ellsworth to connect Iowa Falls to Des Moines, the capital city. Railroads at the time were the most important form of transportation in the nation.

It was in Iowa Falls that Eugene S. Ellsworth founded Ellsworth College in 1890 as a four-year institution, and it proved a popular school from the very beginning. When Sheridan Jones was offered a post teaching at Ellsworth in 1908, it was as part of the college's expansion, and when Jones relocated there he discovered a growing and prosperous town. New building seemed to spring up almost every year to change the Iowa Falls landscape. For example, in 1902 the Illinois Central Depot was constructed on East Pennsylvania, and in 1909 a new bridge was built to span the Iowa River. In 1911, just three years after Sheridan Jones moved to Iowa Falls, the Mills Tower complex was completed on the east side of town. Further city expansion continued throughout the 1910s and 1920s.

Ellsworth College, Iowa Falls Ia., U. S. A.

Ellsworth College, ca. 1910

Today, Iowa Falls has a population of 5,193 and Ellsworth College is now Ellsworth Community College, one of the leading two-year educational institutions in America. There are still a number of people at Ellsworth College and in Iowa City who fondly remember Sheridan Jones.

Chapter 3:

PROFESSOR JONES

Sheridan Ross Jones was head of the biology department and/or Dean of the old Ellsworth and Ellsworth Junior Colleges from 1908 to 1940. Students and friends throughout the community best knew Sheridan as "Prof. Jones," although other nicknames like Doc, Pop, Uncle, Hezzy and Sherry were used less commonly. As described by his former students, Dorothy and Mike Chaplin of Iowa Falls, Sheridan was short in stature with shorter than average arms. He was also quite rotund and was known to mention frequently that he knew he was ready for a diet "when I couldn't bend over and tie my shoes."

Sheridan would always start biology lectures by clearing his throat. Sometimes he would skip biology for the moment and talk about current world events. Sheridan was very likeable and had a wonderful sense of humor, and loved to use the little Audubon Bird Book in class. He taught many other subjects besides biology, such as nature study, human physiology, natural science, heredity and genetics.

When outside the classroom, Sheridan could often be seen chomping on a cigar or fishing just down the road on the Iowa River. His students never knew what to expect or what he might pull out of his pocket: a mouse, rat, shrew, snake or baby bird. The class would dissect angleworms and put them in pickle tubes. They sometimes passed around a garden snake from student to student. The girls especially didn't smile on this, but neither did they refuse.

Sheridan's teaching prowess was legendary at Ellsworth. His motto was "You don't teach subjects, you teach students." He was also a believer in teaching with

Sheridan Jones fishing in the Iowa River.

field trips, using the outdoors as his classroom. One of his students, Harriet Moore was born with one blue and one brown eye, and Sheridan delighted in using her as an example of dominant vs. recessive genes. After an early morning bird hike, he would cook breakfast for his students at his cabin in the woods on the Iowa River.

Sheridan's hilltop cabin was featured in several articles where he wrote about fishing for smallmouth bass in the Iowa River.

Sheridan R. Jones, associate editor of Outdoor Recreation, and noted authority on fishing.

Sheridan was the best kind of teacher in that he could bring a subject alive for the students. Through his great personal experience in the field, Prof. Jones could easily relate to the students of Ellsworth, many of whom were born and raised on farms in the Iowa countryside and by the time they reached college had spent many hours in the field observing nature. One such student was Rich A. Wheeler, MD, who came from the nearby city of Alden and related an interesting story about his former Professor Jones by letter:

"I remember Dean Sheridan Jones very well as my professor of zoology at Ellsworth Junior College when I commuted from our farm near Alden in 1939-40 and 1940-41. He was very well informed and very interesting and kind. One of his anecdotes concerned a very large snapping turtle he had seen. The story, to the best of my knowledge went something like this:

One year a few summers back, two or three times during the summer fishermen came running up from the lake into town, babbling about something they had seen in the water that sounded like an alligator or a dinosaur. Nobody believed them. I saw it too, but I didn't tell anybody because nobody would have believed me, either. However, I will tell you and let you draw your own conclusions. I was fishing for crappies off the icehouse dock, had three or four on a stringer and was sitting there waiting for the next one when I saw some faint, slow motion down below my string of fish. I thought 'Ah, there's about a twenty pound turtle trying to steal my fish. I'll just wait until he gets a little closer and then scare the heck out of him, and that will be the end of it.' I waited a bit and took another look and realized that what I thought was a twenty pound turtle was actually just the head of the turtle. The rest of it extended out into the murky depths and out of sight. It scared me so that I picked up my fishing pole and ran. I didn't make any attempt to rescue my stringer. I wouldn't guess at how big it was. I only know that at first glance, I mistook its head for a twenty pound snapper. Nobody saw it except during that one summer, so I suppose that when the weather cooled off, it made its way back down to the Mississippi where it came from.

After class, he and I discussed the experience. We recalled that in a recent newspaper there had been a picture of a one hundred pound snapping turtle that two men had gotten from the Mississippi, showing what looked like a six or seven foot lizard with a heavy signet ring around its waist – a turtle that size really doesn't need a shell for protection any more – and an inordinately large head, possibly as much as twenty percent of the weight of the entire animal. Prof. thought about that for a moment, then agreed that probably what he had seen was a snapping turtle in the 100-125 pound range, and we chuckled that it certainly was not something that people would want in the same swimming pool with them."

Ellsworth Yule dinner is tradition

IOWA FALLS — The annual Ellsworth College Christmas dinner took place Tuesday evening with more than 500 students, faculty members and guests attending. Guests included members of the Ellsworth College board, members of the board of education of the Iowa Falls Community school district and Mrs. Sheridan Jones.

The dinner was started in the days of the depression and has become a tradition. Ellsworth became a public junior college in 1929, a time when students had a hard time to find enough funds for necessities. A group of students appealed to the late Sheridan Jones, dean of the school, for suggestions for entertainment. He suggested a Christmas dinner before the students left for their homes for the holidays.

It was to be a simple meal with plain food, such as they might have when they went to Grandmother's h o m e. Carol singing and a few short talks made the program.

The women of the Ellis Methodist Church, southwest of Iowa Falls, have prepared and served the meal for many years. One corner of the room is arranged as an oldfashioned room with reed organ, r o c k i n g chair, braided rug, a fireplace.

The Mason City Globe-Gazette reported on the Ellsworth College Yule Dinner, founded over three decades earlier by Sheridan Jones, on 17 Dec. 1964.

In the early years of the Great Depression when students couldn't afford to travel home for Christmas, he instituted a student and faculty Christmas Dinner. This event continues to be celebrated every Christmas time at Ellsworth College. Still, his greatest achievements were in the classroom, where thousands of his students, without a single exception, are better men, women and citizens because they came under his influence. For 48 years (1908-1956) Sheridan R. Jones was the heart and soul of the biology department at Ellsworth College in Iowa Falls, and one of the most popular professors on campus.

Sheridan was a tireless promoter of Ellsworth College, and in fact wore two academic hats for many years as he was also named the Dean of the College. During the hard times of the Great Depression in the 1930s, the college went from a four-year institution to a two-year program, which even included high school classes.

Jones, as dedicated as he was to education, helped to hold the college together during these tough times and even became a college recruiter when tuition paying students were hard to find from the surrounding local towns. He did most of the administrative paperwork by himself until he called Dorothy Chaplin one day and asked her to help as office secretary in exchange for tuition costs to finish her degree which she couldn't otherwise afford.

Sheridan was a popular and respected professor at the college, and his home was always open for students to visit and have tea or coffee and chat. Many of these students would remember Prof. Jones and all that he did for them and their classmates for the rest of their lives. He truly was a legendary figure on the Ellsworth College campus.

"Prof" conducts a science class in the basement of Bullock Jones. Students: table left rear - Betty Goodyear, Karl Bottke, Kenneth Madole. Table down left - Marilyn Hoffman. Table right rear - Dorian Dagit, Jim Hayden, Eugene Heflin; table lower right - Joe Brotherton, Bob Pulis. [Source: ECC Collection]

Numerous displays like this in the Ellsworth College museum were used by Sheridan Jones to help instruct generations of students on the intricacies of nature. Many of the mounts were done by Jones himself.

Moments in History / Places in Time

THE GREAT DEPRESSION

T *he Great Depression began in late October 1929 when the stock market crashed. The stock market lost so much of its value it did not reach pre-1929 levels again until 1954. How catastrophic this economic downturn was can be seen in the fact that on just one day—October 29, 1929, the infamous Black Tuesday—the Dow Jones Industrial lost $14 billion, or 12% of its total value.*

The Depression had its roots in the 1920s when Americans enjoyed booming economic times. The end of World War I brought mass production of consumer products and growth in all economic segments. The automotive, public utilities, and entertainment and recreation industries prospered. Agriculture, real estate, construction, oil refining, banking and finance, and manufacturing of rubber, paper, and consumer products all flourished.

A resident of Dubuque, Iowa's "Shacktown" ca. 1931. Almost every city had tent camps on the outskirts of town where the displaced and homeless lived.

Sheridan Jones was part of the great post-war boom in fishing and fishing tackle. His articles, profiled in the appendix, and his promotion of fishing tackle, detailed in a later chapter, are a testament to the carefree attitude that gave the decade the nickname "The Roaring '20s."

However, the demand for farm products overseas gradually decreased (lowering prices and increasing supplies), industrialization slowed (work hours were cut and jobs lost), and banks made easy loans and credit that increased consumer debt. Few people recognized the early warning signs. For many years corporate stocks rose rapidly in value. Many people purchased stocks on margin in hopes of making quick profits. Then on October 24, 1929, the New York Stock Exchange crashed as billions in paper profits were lost. This signaled the beginning of the longest economic crisis in U.S. and world history, which quickly became known as the Great Depression (1929-1941).

The Depression gripped the whole nation as businesses collapsed and millions lost their jobs. In American cities hundreds of people stood in bread lines

DID YOU KNOW

The invention of the Ford Model T, the first popular mass-produced automobile, changed American life forever. In 1914 the Ford assembly line could turn out a complete chassis every 93 seconds. Henry Ford, the owner of the Ford Motor Company, famously quipped that the customer could order a Model T in any color they liked, as long as it was black.

The Model T was produced until 1927, and Ford sold over 15 million of these cars. Many new roads and highways were built. This opened up the countryside, forest, lakes, rivers and streams for both campers and anglers alike. A new outdoor fishing culture blossomed in America and demanded new and modern camping and angling equipment. It was during this era (1914-1927) when many new firms emerged that mass produced new rods, reels and lures in factories.

for hours, and others sold apples on street corners for a nickel in an effort to earn enough to eat. Many couldn't pay their bills and lost their homes, especially in rural communities where many banks failed. The economy did not recover until the beginning of World War II in 1941.

The 1930s thus became a decade of frustration and fear for Americans. Government relief became the rule instead of the exception, and bread and soup lines could be found in every city and town. Images of the Depression were fixed in American popular memory by writers such as John Steinbeck, whose novel The Grapes of Wrath *is a moving fictional account of life in 1930s America.*

In 1933, newly elected president Franklin D. Roosevelt inaugurated the New Deal, a comprehensive effort to fix the foundering economy. One of these acts, later struck down as unconstitutional by the U.S. Supreme Court, was the National Recovery Act, which set labor laws for every American industry—including the Fishing Tackle Manufacturing Industry. Other New Deal acts such as the Civilian Conservation Corp (CCC) put to work millions of young men in the outdoors constructing local and state parks, clearing forests, etc.

The Great Depression did not come to an end until America's entry into World War II in 1941. It is one of the most important events in American history.

Sheridan Jones' personal Intox-Oreno and Paper Weight were gifts from the South Bend Bait Company. The Intox-Oreno is considered a novelty lure and only a very few exist. It was not a catalog item. The Intox-Oreno is a secret flask designed to hold an alcoholic beverage during the era of Prohibition (1920-1933) when the drinking of alcohol was illegal. The one pictured above was found in Sheridan's collection new and unused, with its original hang tag intact. The Paper Weight with Jones' name has the words "Fish and Feel Fit" on the base, a slogan developed by the American Fishing Tackle Manufacturer's Association in 1926 and utilized by South Bend in most of their subsequent advertising.

Chapter 4:

SHERIDAN'S "OTHER" LIFE

While Sheridan worked full time at the college, most people at Ellsworth College were unaware of his fame and popularity as an angling editor and writer. He kept his fan mail and tackle collection to himself and was modest about his accomplishments as a fishing writer. His articles in *Outer's Book* began in April 1913, during the same time Sheridan had been attending the University of Michigan doing graduate work. He chose a difficult schedule of intensified study of key subjects in the biology fields of Ichthyology, Plant Geography, Comparative Psychology, Genetics, Physiobiology of Maintenance and Reproduction, and Animal Distribution. His prominent instructors were each known nationally for their work in their special fields but they were not what Sheridan wanted to become at a large university. So when the opportunity came for him to stay, he chose to return to Ellsworth College and the clear Iowa River waters in Iowa Falls. It is possible his decision was made easier by the start of World War I and the subsequent thinning ranks of students. Regardless of the reason for his decision, he further developed his other life as a prolific fishing writer while engaged at Ellsworth. One of Sheridan's first submissions to *Outer's* was "Pre-season

SIXTEEN YEARS OF PROMINENCE

Sheridan began writing fishing articles in the National Monthly Magazine *Outer's Book* in April 1913. In April 1918 he became the fishing editor of *Outer's Recreation* when it merged with *Recreation Magazine*.

Then in 1924 *Outers' Recreation* merged with *Outdoor Magazine* to become *Outdoor Recreation*. This magazine eventually merged in *Outdoor Life*, which still remains very popular. Sheridan's last article was in the June 1929 issue of *Outdoor Recreation*.

Privileges and Sporting Tackle." Most of his magazine fishing articles discussed the newest designs and developments in fishing tackle and lures that were the "state of the art" at that time. His writing career was really launched when, in May 1914, his article "My Bacon Winners" for *Outer's Book* won first prize, a reel valued at $22.50, but more importantly attained national recognition.

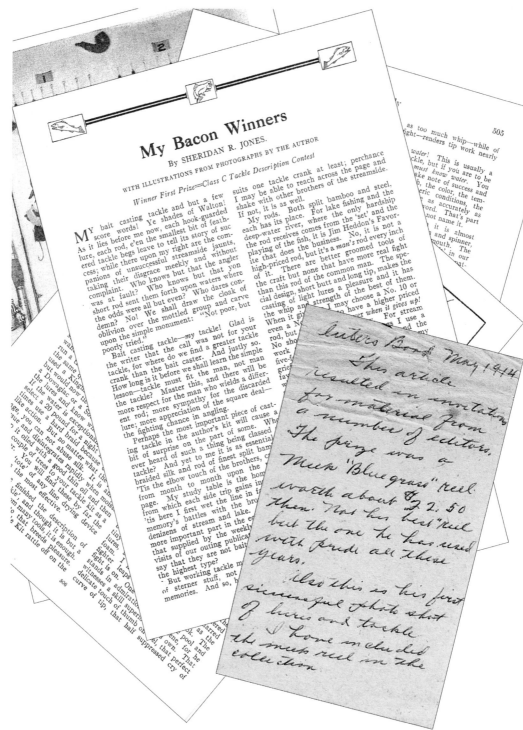

Sheridan Jones' first prize winning essay for Outer's resulted in his winning a valuable Meek casting reel, as evidenced by his wife's handwritten note.

Sheridan Jones began editing Outers Recreation with the April 1918 issue.

Outer's Book grew and changed to *Outer's Recreation Magazine*, and in April 1918 Sheridan R. Jones became its Angling Editor. His first article in the April edition "With Bait and Fly" column was titled, "The Spell of the Curl O'Blue." In this article, Sheridan wrote about the essence of nature—the sounds and smells of the outdoors and woodlands, and the atmosphere of the campfire and campsite. The second article published in this issue was "Black Bass and Bass-Craft: An Introduction." This first column began a series of in-depth articles on tactics and techniques of Bass fishing through the eyes of a scientist, and began to cement Jones' reputation as one of the nation's most preeminent experts on bass angling.

Other articles included:

"Breeding Habits of Black Bass," *Outer's* (June 1919)
"Bass of the Seasons," *Outer's* (June 1920)
"The Smallmouth of the Pools" *Outer's* (July 1919)

Eventually these articles were collected and revised to form the chapters of his best selling book published in 1924 as *Black Bass and Bass Craft* by The Macmillan Company of New York, one of the largest publishing houses in the world. Untold numbers of men, and increasing numbers of women, were introduced to the scientific method of bass angling through Sheridan's articles and book. It ranks today as one of the most important books written on the subject of bass fishing.

23

BLACK BASS &
BASS CRAFT
Sheridan R. Jones
Black Bass a
The Life Habits
and Successful A
By
Sheridan R
Author of
"Fishing Facts," "Bait Casting,"
Angling Editor of Outer
With Photographs and
By the Author
New York
The Macmillan Company
1924
All rights reserved
TENTS
PAGE
vii
ix
ING BOG 1
GE-MOUTH) 7
WATERS 15
F THE RUSHES 24
WEED BEDS 30
UTH 39
E RIVER 48
L-MOUTH 56
HE LEDGES 61
THE POOLS 69
TE WATERS 78
85
XIII BASS OF THE SEASONS 92
XIV BASS OF MANY WATERS 99
XV THE BREEDING HABITS OF BLACK BASS 107
XVI ANGLING METHODS ON BLOOMING WATERS 118
XVII MAY WATERS AND BASS BAITS 125
XVIII LOCAL COLOR AND ARTIFICIAL BAITS 133
XIX YE ANGLER OF THE NIGHT-LINE 145
XX PLAYING FROM THE REEL 155
XXI THE SPLASH OR THE SILENT CAST 161
XXII CAN BASS DISTINGUISH COLORS? 171
XXIII BLACK AS A LURE COLOR 179
XXIV CAN BASS HEAR? 185
XXV NATURAL LURES FOR BASS 192

Sheridan Jones' Book Black Bass & Bass Craft (1924)
From Top Left: Personaliztion; Frontispiece, Title Page, Contents.

Black Bass and Bass Craft was one of the most authoritative resources for bass fisherman during its time. It helped create interest in bass fishing with insights into the science of bass fishing. Its chapters contained information on black bass, differing characteristics amongst species of bass, their habits according to different bodies of water, and baits and lures appropriate for various conditions. There are especially fine chapters on lures, tackle, casting methods, and reel use. This book received national recognition as being one of the first presentations for the

DID YOU KNOW?

From 1920 to 1927 *Outer's Recreation* combined with *Field & Stream* to publish an Annual Sporting Magazine issue *Vacation Manual*. The most popular sporting writers, including Sheridan Jones, were invited to contribute articles.

layman in its scientific field and it was later put into foreign publication. The previous authoritative treatise on the bass fishing was *The Book of Black Bass* by Dr. James Alexander Henshall, published first in 1881 and then republished multiple times up to 1939.

In 1920, Sheridan Jones became full angling editor of *Outdoor Recreation's* annual publication *Vacation Manual*. In the 1921 *Vacation Manual* article "Lines and Lures of All Sorts," Sheridan writes that lures with double hooks are more than sufficient and weedless lures are very useful and effective,

saying "Beware of multi-hooked offerings." It seems he had plenty of compassion for the fish and felt these water creatures should be given a sporting chance. In the Appendix you will find reproduced copies of the articles "Tools for Bait-Casting Craft" (1920), "Long Distance and Short Rods" (1924), "The Short Rod's Possibilities" (1925) and "The Motor You Need" (1927).

In the 1924 *Vacation Manual* article Sheridan writes, "Fish not so much to catch fish as to learn to catch them. It's the easiest thing in the world to take bass and lunge from virgin waters. But to take one bass when other anglers draw a blank; to take him

The
Outlook
An Illustrated Weekly Journal of Current Events

*Annual
Out-of-Doors
Number*

The America's Cup Once More
By W. J. Henderson

How to Set Up a Camp
By Mary A. Hopkins

After the War Travel in Europa
by E. F. Baldwin

A Maine Seacoast Village
Eight Photographs by Henry Hoyt Moore

Bird Hunting With a Camera
By Dr. Arthur A. Allen

WEDNESDAY, JUNE 9, 1920
PRICE: FIFTEEN CENTS A COPY
FIVE DOLLARS A YEAR
381 FOURTH AVENUE, NEW YORK

ON THE WAY TO ICEBERG LAKE IN THE GLACIER
MOUNTAIN PARK, MONTANA

because you have tried out every depth of water, every type of lure action, every form of offering from plug to spinner; then to offer on the altar of the Reel Gods your last sacrifice, a last hope as the shadows dim the shoreline – to take him then, to finally solve the mystery of his mood – that, and that alone, will crown the angler's brow with sweet content."

In 1920, Sheridan also began freelance writing for *Outlook* magazine edited by Teddy Roosevelt and the popular journal *Field and Stream*. His first article appeared on June 9, 1920 and was entitled "On an Angling Chord or a Twisted String." Sheridan felt that anglers should take the lead in the spirit of brotherhood of men and return all unneeded fish back to the water. He wrote about how the greed of mankind could result in an angling chord of just a memory for future generations.

The most popular and widely distributed books written by Sheridan Jones were the soft cover titles *Bait Casting, Fishing Facts* and *Fly Casting*. Selling thousands of copies annually, these three handy 80 page pocket booklets were part of a recreation library advertised in most sporting magazines at the time, and could be ordered by readers with a magazine coupon for 25¢ each. They were full of practical information; in *Fishing Facts*, for example, he wrote "did you know that the night crawlers, *Allolobrophora Foetida* to the brethren in the know, come out at night to feed upon the softer parts of decaying vegetation?"

Sheridan Jones also wrote feature articles for the South Bend Bait Company in their 1924 and 1925 *Pocket Tackle Catalogs*. In one such article, "Crappie, Bluegill and Rock Bass on Artificial Baits" he wrote "we've had enough of slimy worms, of clammy frogs, of sickly minnows, for we can take our share and move with dainty artificial baits – and on a long cane pole!" South Bend Bait Company was particularly fond of Sheridan and sent him plenty of lures, reels and poles, and even an engraved Bass Oreno paperweight with his signature on the lure. They also made for him what is certainly one of only a few known Intox-Orenos, a Bass-Oreno with a screw off head that made a handy medicine or liquor flask.

These three titles (red) were written by Sheridan Jones and copyrighted (1923)
by Outer's Book Company and Outdoor Life (1927).
Bottom right is 1927 South Bend Catalog..

Sheridan wrote extensively about the art of bait casting which was in its infancy in the early 20th century America. One famous lure company, The Hastings Sporting Goods Works of Hasting, Michigan, made the then popular Wilson Wobbler lures. These were wooden lures with fluted or indented noses that created wobbles in the water when retrieved. Sheridan Jones authored *Bait Casting*, a sixteen page booklet that Hastings Sporting Goods distributed in 1916. He wrote:

We strongly advise heading your list with the fluted wobbler—the wobbler that all the old timers tie to and the one which all others are judged. Wilson Wobblers are all built on the disabled minnow principle—the natural food of game fish everywhere and for this reason are effective when other lures fail. The prime essential in an artificial casting lure is that it shall emulate in form or motion the erratic action of a disabled minnow. The old type of underwater minnow was not satisfactory unless manipulated by the rod tip and reel in a manner suggestive of the wobbling flight of a crippled shiner. The difficulty encountered here produced the fluted wobbler—the most deadly article lure yet devised. Fished day in and day out, season in and season out, the fluted wobbler will score a grand total unapproached by any other lure. There is but one indictment against the fluted wobbler—it is too deadly!

The Johnson Motor Co. of South Bend, Indiana, which was the world's leader of outboard boat motor sales at the time, published *A Guide to Waterways Travels*. This softbound 187-page book was filled with stories and maps of trips outdoorsman and vacationers could undertake in America's waterways and the Canadian provinces. Sheridan's article in this booklet "The Fisherman and His

Correspondence between the Johnson Motor Company and Jones.

Outboard Motor" was very complimentary about his own 1925 Johnson Outboard and the events of his own fishing trips during the summer of 1925. His enthusiasm for motor boating also led him to organize the first boat club on the Iowa River right in Iowa Falls, a short walk down the hill from his home on Pierce Street. The club's building still stands today on the edge of the Iowa River with the same character and charm of a backwoods lodge that was exactly to Sheridan's liking.

The several dozen articles he wrote for the monthly issues of *Outdoor Recreation* on the "Freshwater Angler" discussed the food chain in streams, ponds, rivers and lakes. They were not only about the fish, but about the complete life cycle of the water bodies and their inherent species such as crayfish, algae, plants, larvae, insects, worms, minnows, frogs, fly crustaceans and diatoms, and how all were part of the food chain and total eco-system. Each article was complete with many of his artistic diagrams and illustrations of all freshwater game fish species.

Angling Department

CONDUCTED BY

Sheridan R. Jones & O.W. Smith

Greetings From Ye Editor

An Announcement

HOWDY, everybody! And mighty glad to be saying it, too! Wish we could just give every one of you fellows a friendly wallop in the middle of the back and put a little pep into the old casting arm with a few real handshakes. That's just the way we feel about it—and why shouldn't we, with all the boys from Outdoor Recreation joining forces with you fellows and the whole bunch of us headed straight down the trail together. Fellows, meet each other; fill up the jimmy pipes and swap a few yarns —that'll give us a chance to get our breath and to do a little serious thinking about this business of being *Fishing Editor* of the NEW OUTDOOR LIFE.

And that's no joke about being out of breath. Here we were, taking a perfectly harmless fishing trip into the Ozarks and the "powers that be" nearly wrecked our whole vacation trying to collar us for a little work on the new magazine. Of

Sheridan R. Jones

course we said we'd do it and then, when they weren't looking, we snook away into the North Woods for the big bass opening up there— and didn't leave any address! Of course we had to come back *sometime,* and they sure landed on us when we did get within reach of the air mail and the telegraph. Had a wonderful time in the Ozarks and grand bass fishing up north; but I guess we're back in time to say "howdy" and to tell you that we're chock full of fishing dope and that from now on we're strictly on the job with Outdoor Life!

We're mighty glad that Outdoor Recreation and Outdoor Life have at last joined hands, and mighty proud to serve as Angling Editor of the new publication. We've a lot of good things planned for the coming months, but

first we must say "howdy" and "how's fishin' been?"
Heartily,
SHERIDAN R. JONES,
Formerly Angling Editor of Outdoor Recreation.

When Outer's Recreation merged with Outdoor Life, Sheridan Jones became
fishing editor and published this notice.

His enthusiasm and expertise in science and angling were evident in all his published articles. Some of the more popular from *Outer's Book* and *Outers Recreation* include: "Ye Angler of the Night-Line" (June 1916), "Efficient Bait Casting Lines" (July 1914), "How Well Do Fish Hear?" (January 1922), "The Pikes in October" (October 1921), and "Fishing Accessories" (October 1920).

In *Outdoor Life* and *Outdoor Recreation* combined, several of his popular articles were: "Midsummer Trolling" (September 1928), "Shore Fishing for Bass" (October 1928), "Selecting a Lure" (November 1928), "Spoons, Spinners and Metal Attractors" (March 1929), "The Casting Plug" (June 1929), and "Enameled Metal Casting Lure" (May 1929).

THE CALL of THE OUTDOORS
by Will H. Dilg
PRESIDENT. I.W.L.A.

ANGLERS, WET YOUR HANDS.

"All fish should be handled with moist hands to guard against removing the body slime. Slime is a natural protection against fungus, and a scraped portion may result in an infection causing the death of the fish," says a noted authority, Sheridan R. Jones.

Will Dilg of Chicago often cited Sheridan Jones in his syndicated column. Dilg was co-founder and president of the famous Isaac Walton League, a pioneering environmental organization.

In the 1920s in America *Outer's Recreation* magazine printed more stories and articles on fishing than any other publication in the country, and clearly Sheridan Jones was a motivating factor behind this. He was greatly respected both by the common angler and by other fishing writers; as one of his fellow outdoor writers declared, "In practical experience with tackle and in sound fish getting lore, it can be stated with positive assurance that Sheridan R. Jones is the peer of any expert in the country." His angling articles were as authoritative as they were enjoyable and many were syndicated to daily American newspapers. Jones was a respected figure within the community of outdoor journalists and trailblazing environmentalists. He was renowned as an angling expert of his time because of his experience and his ability to present practical information in a readable and enjoyable format without sacrificing the scientific angle.

Moments in History / Places in Time

THE ROARING '20S

They called the decade after World War I the "Roaring '20s" because of the prosperous economic conditions that positively affected nearly all Americans. Weary of war, many Americans began to seek an escape from the realities of the world in literature, film, and especially radio—inaugurated in 1922 and soon after available in every major city.

The Jazz Age, as it was also called, gave us the famed baseball slugger Babe Ruth, silent film star Charlie Chaplin, boxer Jack Dempsey, jazz legend Louis Armstrong, and writer F. Scott Fitzgerald, whose main character in the novel The Great Gatsby came to symbolize the era.

Angling rose to new heights, and Sheridan Jones was one of the nation's prominent outdoor writers of the Roaring '20s. The fishing and outdoor lifestyle were encouraged throughout the nation, and the slogan "Fish and Feel Fit"—coined by the Fishing Tackle Manufacturer's Association (FTMA)—was widely promoted, particularly by the South Bend Bait Company of South Bend, Indiana.

Existing companies rapidly expanded, and numerous fishing tackle manufacturers were formed to fill the growing demands of the American angler. The earning power of the average American rose every year between 1920 and 1929, and Americans embraced the new and novel in increasing numbers. Henry Ford's Model T, the first mass-produced car in history, changed American society in tangible ways. From young women known as Flappers, who shocked their elders with their dramatic style of dress, to the returning soldiers who formed the first motorcycle clubs, America seemed constantly on the move.

The truth, however, is that from our perspective we can see the 1920s as a calm before the storm, as the Great Depression silently waited to burst the dam of prosperity. It would change almost every American's life, including Sheridan Jones.

Chapter 5:

SHERIDAN JONES' LURE LEGACY

The greatest tangible treasure that remains from Sheridan's legacy is his extensive collection of fishing lures. Many of America's first artificial lure manufacturing companies were blossoming in the 1910s and 1920s. Their new lures were sent to Sheridan in hope that he would approve and write about them. His mailbox on the front porch wall of 916 Pierce Street was large enough to receive all the packages from the fishing tackle companies. Sheridan would sit in the sofa rocking chair next to the mail chute inside his living room in anticipation of the next delivery of newly designed and constructed fishing lures and tackle. They came directly from the lure companies and were handcrafted and often made one at a time. They were shaped mostly from wood or metal, coated with primer, paint and varnish, and with shiny new hooks attached in various hardware configurations.

The new lures were all individually packaged and put in two-piece cardboard boxes with complete information sheets and instructions for their successful use. These boxes usually had the new company's labels, but a few first off the line lures from the Jamison Company had unique handwritten manuscript labels. Incidentally, the large wall mailbox on the porch is still preserved today by the house's current owners, Bob and Deb Anders.

Sheridan Jones probably didn't receive cash for his endorsements the way many similar experts in the field of sports might receive it today. His reward was free products and national acclaim. The heavy competition amongst the lure companies to perfect the artificial fishing lure led

Sheridan Jones' large wall mailbox was often filled with fishing tackle sent by manufacturers.

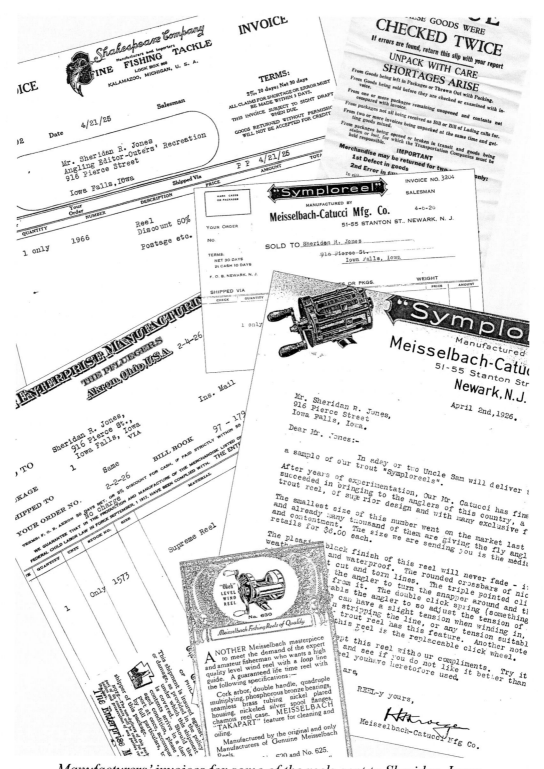

Manufacturers' invoices for some of the reels sent to Sheridan Jones.

to multiple lawsuits among them for patent infringements that may have involved many aspects of the design, size, shape, hardware, and distinct features each lure possessed.

Sheridan's lure collection came from several dozen different companies, with many various patterns, colors, shapes and sizes. His personal tackle boxes were also featured in several of his major articles as well as these promotional lures and tackle. Sheridan accumulated hundred of lures between 1910 and 1930, sent by the fishing lure manufacturers in hopes of his endorsement. They came in cardboard boxes with manufacturer's paperwork and instructions.

In three *Outer's Book* articles—"Some Plug Dope for the Amateur Bait-Caster" (December 1914), "The 1915 Baits–A Tackle Screed in Two Casts," (April 1915), and "Looking 'Em Over for 1916," (May 1916)—the exact lures pictured in these articles were found in his lure collection. In these articles (and others) Sheridan discusses their fish-catching value in terms of their construction, size, colors, hook points, the commotion they can make, and manufacturer claims. He used his wealth of scientific knowledge on fish, habitats, bodies of water, natural feed and his own angling techniques and expertise to analyze these new developments.

One new lure discussed in the 1916 article was a "real-like" gray mouse New Redfin No. 77 that was advertised in the same issue. Sheridan stated that its unique hook hangers were a real mouthful and made by James L. Donaly Company, Newark, New Jersey.

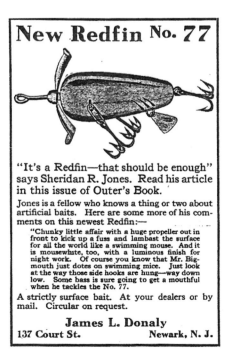

New Redfin No. 77

"It's a Redfin—that should be enough" says Sheridan R. Jones. Read his article in this issue of Outer's Book.

Jones is a fellow who knows a thing or two about artificial baits. Here are some more of his comments on this newest Redfin:—

"Chunky little affair with a huge propeller out in front to kick up a fuss and lambast the surface for all the world like a swimming mouse. And it is mousewhite, too, with a luminous finish for night work. Of course you know that Mr. Bigmouth just dotes on swimming mice. Just look at the way those side hooks are hung—way down low. Some bass is sure going to get a mouthful when he tackles the No. 77.

A strictly surface bait. At your dealers or by mail. Circular on request.

James L. Donaly
137 Court St.   Newark, N. J.

Sheridan categorized artificial lures as surface, near surface, and underwater, with the best sellers being wobblers, wigglers, dancers and divers. In his *Outer's Book and Recreation* monthly fishing column "With Bait and Fly," Sheridan Jones discussed not only the current state of the art in new lures, reels, and rods, but also all about the art of fishing techniques. All the freshwater sport fishing species were studied with insights into their favorite habitats, feed and feeding cycles, and best methods for catching them.

The Coming of the Clan

Just a Wee Glimpse at Some of the Opening Day Favorites

By SHERIDAN R. JONES

ILLUSTRATIONS FROM PHOTOGRAPHS BY THE AUTHOR

Al Foss Pork Rind Minnow

The Tango Surface Midget

The Moonlight Ladybug Wiggler

Jamison's New Struggling Mouse

Angling
conducted by
Sheridan R. Jones

The Casting Plug

By Sheridan R. Jones

Part I

A group of easy swimmers

Surface plugs for weedy waters

Odd shapes are often used to get action

Outers' Recreation

With Bait and Fly

Edited by SHERIDAN R. JONES

More on Fishing Accessories
Weedless Hooks and Weedless Lures

By Sheridan R. Jones

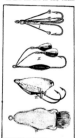

Outdoor Recreation

On the Tackle Counter

By Sheridan R. Jones

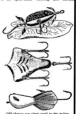

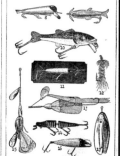

Sheridan Jones wrote extensively on the latest fishing tackle. He was so respected that his endorsement often helped the sales of new lures.

A Creek Chub Pikie Minnow (1919) in an introductory box with paperwork, from the Sheridan Jones Lure Collection. The Creek Chub Bait Company of Garrett, Indiana, sold over 44,000,000 Pikie Minnows in the course of its production run.

Moments in History / Places in Time

CELEBRITY ENDORSEMENTS

Today we are accustomed to celebrity endorsements; indeed, it is hard to find a commercial product that is not attached to a famous athlete or Hollywood celebrity

Just like today, during Sheridan Jones' lifetime, celebrity endorsements were the norm. This advertising technique was first popularized in the 1880s, when Henry Slocumb, fresh off victory in the U.S. Open Tennis tournament, endorsed a line of racquets named in his honor for Chicago's A.G. Spalding & Bros. company. By the 1910s and 1920s almost every major manufacturer sought the endorsement of a noted authority or famous star.

This was as true in the fishing tackle industry as it was anywhere else, and one of the most sought after endorsements came from Sheridan R. Jones. Jones' endorsement in print often translated into increased sales, and in the very competitive tackle market, could mean the difference between a success and a failure.

Here's One Paragraph of Mr. Sheridan R. Jones' letter to us of March 4th, 1922—After he had seen "Hildebrandt's Hints."

"Had an opportunity to glance through your "Hints," a copy of which one of the local fishermen had already received, and noted with interest that you had made use of a letter of mine showing what I think of spinners and flies in connection with the small-mouthed bass. No doubt you read between the lines that I was talking about Hildebrandt Spinners. I might have gone farther and stated that your three shapes, Slim Eli, Standard and Idaho, in your various finishes, should always be in the fly-angler's kit. And, if but one of these could be had, it needs must be the Idaho---than which there is no better small-mouth spoon made. I do practically all my small-mouth fishing now-a-days with the fly-rod and spinners in the smaller sizes and must say that they are great killers."

(Mr. Jones is in charge of the angling department of Outers-Recreation magazine.)

Jones took his job as a tester of lures seriously, and did not endorse anything that he felt was unworthy of being associated with his name. It is a testament to his ability to judge a lure's effectiveness that most of the lures he endorsed were manufactured for many years after, and some are still being made today. The truth was that Sheridan Jones understood what caught fish.

What Sheridan R. Jones Says About Spinners

"YOUR letter brings up the old question about the most taking bait day in and day out for small-mouthed bass. While volumes might be prepared for and against the several baits that appeal, at times, to the bronze-back, we have reduced the number to a single offering that will take small-mouthed bass for us with greater regularity than any other individual bait — and this is the small spinner and fly via the fly rod

"Do not understand us to mean that this offering is the most killing at all times. But we will fish it against any and all kinds of bait, both natural and artificial, from the opening of the season until the very last day, and take a better average for every week of the season than any other single offering can show. We believe in this bait for small-mouth. We would not wish to be forced to use it exclusively, yet we would have a pretty good time fishing if such were the case — and we would have fish in the pan at that.

"The older we get in an angling way, the more we are convinced that it is not so much the lure as it is the manner of presenting it that spells success or failure. It is one thing to pull a spinner through the water, it is quite another matter to make it fairly seem a real, living, darting bit of animation. The expert puts his soul into that bit of metal and his success is not the result of a day's casting — it is the result of a complete mastery of that tiny revolving blade."

Manufacturers like the John J. Hildebrandt Company of Logansport, Indiana often reprinted his testimony in their catalogs, the top one from their 1922 edition and the bottom from their 1925 catalog.

Chapter 6:

THE MAN WHO DISAPPEARED

When Robert Page Lincoln wrote in the 1950s about Sheridan R. Jones as the man who suddenly dropped off the face of the earth, it was likely because Sheridan's priority laid with Ellsworth College and the many hats he wore during the Depression years —Dean, Professor, Teacher, Recruiter, Secretary and of course, Husband. His articles ceased in the June 1929 edition of *Outdoor Recreation* and his colleagues and students only knew him as "Prof" and not necessarily for his national recognition as America's Fishing Tackle Guru. He was dedicated to assisting his students in real life as well as in the classroom and was so likeable that his students and friends gravitated to him.

Jones' students spent many hours studying at the Ellsworth College Library, now known as Bullock Jones Hall. Sheridan Jones spent much of his teaching career in this building.

Sheridan's first wife Mae died at a young age and he was remarried to Vivian Klemme Eller, the daughter of the man for whom an Iowa town was named, in 1928. They had two sons, Donn Jones, who was a career Air Force officer, and Klemme Jones, who was a marine engineer. Both sons were from Vivian's previous marriage and were adopted by Sheridan. Vivian was the town librarian in Iowa Falls for many years.

Sheridan Jones' house was at 916 Pierce Street.

They lived on 916 Pierce Street in Iowa Falls, which was just around the corner from the Ellsworth College Campus and Sheridan's biology laboratory. The Iowa River was a short walk down the hill from his home and full of Smallmouth Bass. During the summer vacation months when he was free from teaching duties, there were trips north to Minnesota and Wisconsin lakes for Largemouth Bass, Northern Pike, Walleye and Muskellunge. Their home was what you might expect of a biology professor with a lot of shrubs and trees (Huckleberry and Buckeye) and plants and flowers that would attract wildlife and birds. Sometimes Sheridan was frowned upon by his neighbors because of the unpleasant smell of dead pheasants from his hunting trips on the river flats and Iowa cornfields. Hanging recently deceased pheasants and ducks on or near the house was the popular method for curing the meat before the bird was feathered and butchered.

The Jones garden was also something to behold. Sheridan loved to garden and wrote an article for *Better Homes and Gardens Magazine*, "Garden Onions that are Better." In other articles about gardening, Sheridan wrote about

DID YOU KNOW?

Better Homes & Gardens, the journal that published Jones' gardening articles, was one of the most widely circulated magazines in America?

growing the unusual. In this article about onions, he said his father planted red onion sets because it was believed that there was special virtue in onions, especially when the sets were red.

In August 1956 a city-wide banquet was organized in Sheridan's honor in Iowa Falls with his students, colleagues, former students, friends, relatives and family members attending. There was a tribute to him in the style of the then popular TV show of the 1950s, "This is Your Life, Sheridan Jones!" It was said that "Sheridan R. Jones, you are the traditions, the heart, the soul, the past, and the future of Ellsworth College. Through thick and thin you stayed with Ellsworth, mostly underpaid but not without friends, and without whom the college might not have carried on."

A photo taken at the time of Jones' retirement.

This citywide Professor Jones Night marked his 75th birthday. He received a three page letter of congratulations from his former teacher, Dr. Lewis Akely, 94 years old, who was still teaching some classes at the University of South Dakota at the time. Sheridan said, "I wouldn't trade one of the last few years, for any one of my boyhood life. Working with youngsters, you just can't get any older than they are. It has been wonderful and I've loved it."

Sheridan's wife Vivian and son Klem Jones were honored in the mid-1980s by being named grand marshalls of the Ellsworth College Homecoming Parade.

When Sheridan R. Jones passed away 18 months later, at home and of congestive heart failure in 1958, he left a beautiful legacy of influence on the thousands of students he reached in the classroom, admiration from the many thousands of fisherman he enlightened and educated in the sport of freshwater fishing and a spectacular, one of a kind lure collection.

In the 1980s, Sheridan's wife Vivian Jones served on the Ellsworth Board of Trustees and after her death in 1999 at the age of 105, she donated her home in Des Moines as a gift to the college. Vivian and son Klemme were the Grand Marshalls during a Homecoming Parade in Iowa Falls for the college. Today, both Donn and Klemme have passed away, but there remain three grandchildren. At Ellsworth College there is a scholarship fund in Sheridan R. Jones' memory that provides monies annually for deserving biology students wishing to attend Ellsworth College in Iowa Falls.

A visit to the Dean's office at Ellsworth College today will produce a picture of the past. A cabinet is filled with Sheridan Jones memorabilia that exemplifies the high esteem he is held in even today in Iowa Falls. Sheridan and his wife Vivian are both buried in a picturesque Iowa Falls cemetery on the hill between the school he called home and the Iowa River where he spent so many hours of tranquil fishing time.

Sheridan had a rare combination of the scientific knowledge of a biologist and naturalist, with the actual fishing experience of a professional angler. The breadth of his articles and his career as an educator made Sheridan R. Jones a remarkable figure in American history. There are few people who get to do all that they love in life but Sheridan Jones seemed to do more than anyone could ever hope for in his lifetime. He serves as a wonderful example of someone who followed their heart and let it lead them to a lifetime of happiness and good works.

The search for the perfect fishing lure is exactly what Sheridan Jones wrote about for years, and the truth is that this search continues still today. It is choosing the exact right offering at any given

The Ellsworth College dean's office contains this cabinet of Sheridan Jones memorabilia.

moment that can bring the fisherman a successful catch. As Sheridan might tell you, carry several dozen lure varieties in your tackle box because you never know which one will be perfect for the moment, or when you might be in immediate need of an extra one!

Sheridan R. Jones' legacy as an educator, naturalist, professional writer, and world-class angler is worthy of remembrance today. He stands as one of the titans in the field of angling writers, and yet his true legacy is felt in the thousands of students he touched in both small and large ways at the small college he loved so much in Iowa Falls, Iowa. To Sheridan Jones at least, this was his *true* legacy.

Sheridan and Vivian Jones' final resting spot:
a gentling sloping hill in an Iowa Falls cemetery.

Moments in History / Places in Time

THE POST-WAR BOOM

W hen the Second World War ended in August 1945, the various branches of the Armed Services contained over 12 million American men and women. With the war over, these soldiers were rapidly discharged and inaugurated what historians refer to as the Post-War Boom. Initially felt in two areas—housing and education—returning soldiers flocked to the suburbs and brought about a massive population shift, with entire cities being built in the pastures and farmlands surrounding most American cities and towns.

Additionally, as returning soldiers were eligible for the G.I. Bill, which paid for their college educations, unprecedented numbers attended college. Many received specialized training in business, engineering, and science and went off to found new companies in the rapidly growing economy.

Dozens of angling publications sprang up in post-war America, including *The Fishing Tackle Digest*, a survey of all available fishing tackle in America.

Nowhere was this boom felt more fully than in sports and recreation. The sport of fishing grew at a phenomenal rate, doubling the number of registered anglers in just a decade. This in turn gave rise to a massive expansion in the fishing tackle industry, but interestingly enough, many of the established firms were left out in the cold as new fishing techniques, such as spinfishing, replaced older ones like fly fishing and bait casting. Many established firms that Jones had extolled in the 1920s slowly faded away.

It is interesting to note that Sheridan R. Jones, who was one of the most important voices in the last boom period in American fishing—the 1920s—watched this all unfold with nary a comment. The truth is that Jones was too committed to both his life as an educator and to his students at Ellsworth College to restart his career as an outdoor writer.

Chapter 7:

THE SHERIDAN R. JONES LURE COLLECTION

As noted, Sheridan R. Jones was perhaps the most important evaluator of fishing lures in the country during his active career in the 1910s and 1920s as an outdoor writer. His search for the "Perfect Lure" led many fishing tackle companies to send their products directly to him for testing, evaluation, and hopefully, an endorsement. These companies would often send him several of the same lures in different colors.

Because of this, during his lifetime Jones accumulated hundreds of fishing lures. As he had his own favorites—based on past fishing experiences—both in manufacturers and lure colors, many of these lures were never used or used only once or twice. Thus when the author purchased the Sheridan R. Jones Lure Collection intact in 1997, there were nearly 300 lures found new in the box. Many of these were introductory boxes for new models and retained their original paperwork. In a few instances, hand-written notes from the factory were included to help Jones understand how the lure was supposed to be fished.

The Jones Lure Collection has been called in print "the finest collection of pre-1925 lures of all time." Its historical importance cannot be underestimated, as it is likely the only opportunity we will ever have to not only see some of these lures mint in their introductory boxes, but also get a window into the nature of the fishing tackle industry during Jones' heyday as an outdoor writer.

There are far too many lures in the Jones Collection to profile in this book, so instead what follows is an annotated selection of some of the more interesting and important lures sent to him for evaluation. Additionally, other fishing tackle items of Sheridan Jones are included, ranging from his personal outboard motor to a Glass Minnow Trap sent to him by the Orvis Company.

Personally owned examples of lures from all the major tackle companies referenced in the past sections are included, as well as a compliment of fly rod lures and a selection of lures from miscellaneous manufacturers. Some of these exact lures were pictured in magazine articles Jones wrote over 90 years ago. The author hopes to write a future volume chronicling all of the lures in the Sheridan R. Jones Lure Collection.

From top to bottom: Creek Chub #100 Wiggler, Jamison Winged Mascot, Heddon Baby Tadpolly, and South Bend Bass-Oreno. These are the EXACT lures pictured in Jones' article "Deluxe New Scale Finish" reprinted in the Appendix.

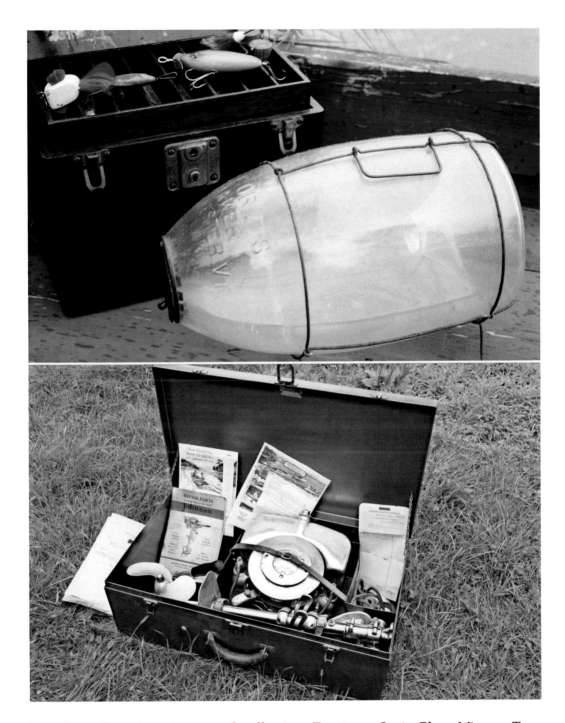

Two items from Jones' personal collection. Top is an Orvis Glass Minnow Trap used to capture live bait, and the bottom is his Johnson Outboard Motor complete with carrying case and operation manuals.

The top pictures a Jamison Co. "Sheridan R. Jones Dark Underwing Moth" named after the author whom they respected so much. On the bottom is a collection of other Jamison fly rod bass bugs and flies. Note the bottom flies are tied to Jamison's patented barbless hook for easy catch-and-release.

The top photo shows two Charles Lane of Madrid, New York lures, on the left a Baby Wagtail Wobbler (1924) and on the right an Automatic Minnow (1913). The bottom photo pictures a collection of Welles patent baits (1913) in a variety of colors and sizes.

(Top) A collection of Jamison casting lures, including the famed Coaxer bait and Shannon twin spinners, the predecessor of today's popular spinnerbaits. (Bottom Left) is a collection of four Moonlight Bait Company feathered fly rod minnows in several styles, ca. 1926. (Bottom Right) A Moonlight Musky Pikaroon.

Sheridan Jones particularly liked South Bend fly rod baits, as evidenced by the large collection above. Below is a selection of the popular E.H. Peckinpaugh feathered minnows, bass bugs, flies, and catalogs.

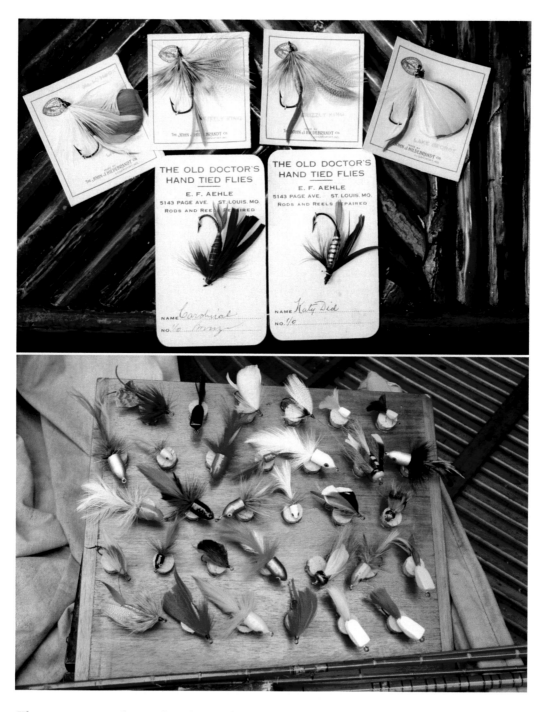

The top picture shows four beautiful John J. Hildebrandt bass flies on cards and two E.F. Aehle "Old Doctor's" hand tied flies. The bottom shows part of Sheridan Jones' fly rod lure tackle box, including a selection from most of the major fly rod lure manufacturers of the era.

Four awesome examples of Creek Chub Bait Company's first fishing lure: the #100 Wiggler, complete with original boxes and paper catalog inserts.

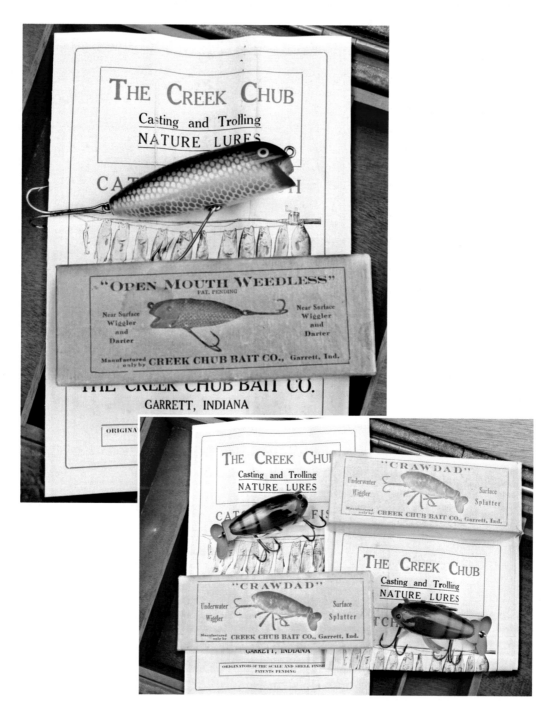

(Top) An extremely rare Creek Chub #500 "Open Mouth Shiner" in its blue introductory box. Note that this lure has painted eyes and is in Red Side Chub color. Ca. 1919. (Bottom) A pair of Creek Chub #400 Crawdads; on the left a #403 River Peeler color and on the right a #402 in Tan Crawdad. Ca. 1919.

Two South Bend lures in "Yellow Hex" color ca. 1919. On the top is a South Bend Underwater Minnow and on the bottom is a South Bend Combination Minnow in "Yellow Hex" with dressed bucktail treble, hand-painted gill marks, and unmarked propellers.

Two South Bend Underwater Minnows. The top shows a model in striking early Perch finish, and on the bottom is an example in a beautiful Frog Spot color.

A frequent find in many old tackle boxes is the Pflueger Globe wooden rotary-head casting lure, ca. 1912. It is similar to the early casting plug invented by Ans. B. Decker of Lake Hopatcong, New Jersey and pictured earlier. This popular bass bait was originally made in Yellow and Gold with Black Spots and Red Head/White colors. This is Sheridan Jones' "Lunker Plug" and shows lots of use, evidence that it was one of his favorite lures and that it caught fish. Pictured in the background is the always popular Pflueger Akron quadruple multiplying casting reel with box and operating manual. The Akron was one of the most popular reels of the era, with jeweled oil cups and in an attractive "polished diamolite" finish.

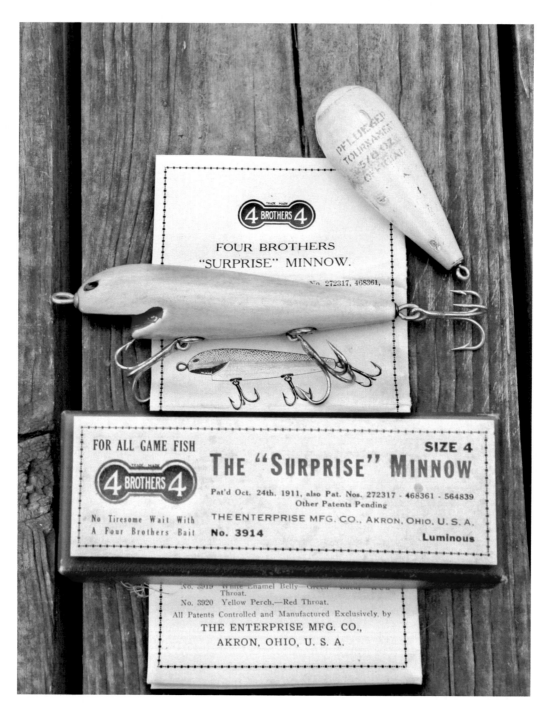

This Pflueger "4 Brothers" Surprise Minnow ca. 1915 in Luminous Finish is the only mint Pflueger lure in the Sheridan Jones Lure Collection—he used all the others! It is pictured with an early Pflueger casting weight.

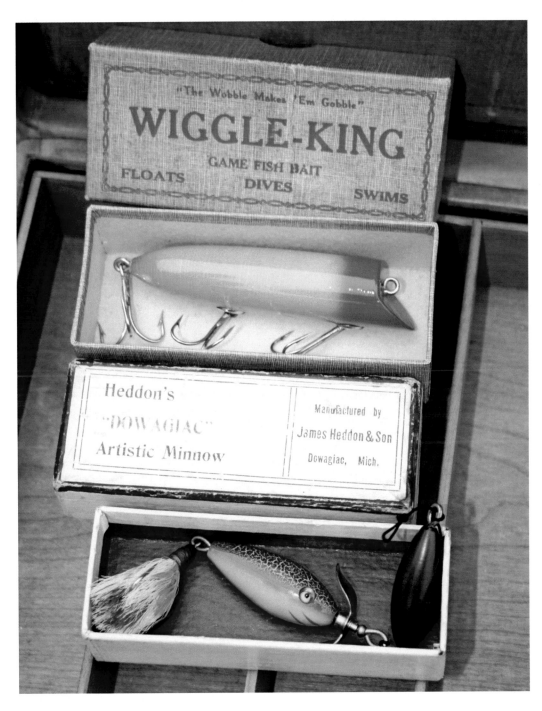

A pair of classic Heddon lures. On top is a Model #2000 Wiggle King lure in Red and White ca. 1918. This lure design transformed in later years into a trio of famous Heddon lures: the Lucky 13, Basser, and Zig-Wag. On the bottom is a #50 Artistic Minnow complete with casting buoy in gorgeous Sienna Crackleback.

A selection of Heddon #1800 Crab Wigglers. The top picture shows three lures with introductory cards, while the bottom shows an exemplary White model with red blush around the eyes and unique hand-painted gill marks indicating it as the earliest of the Crab Wigglers.

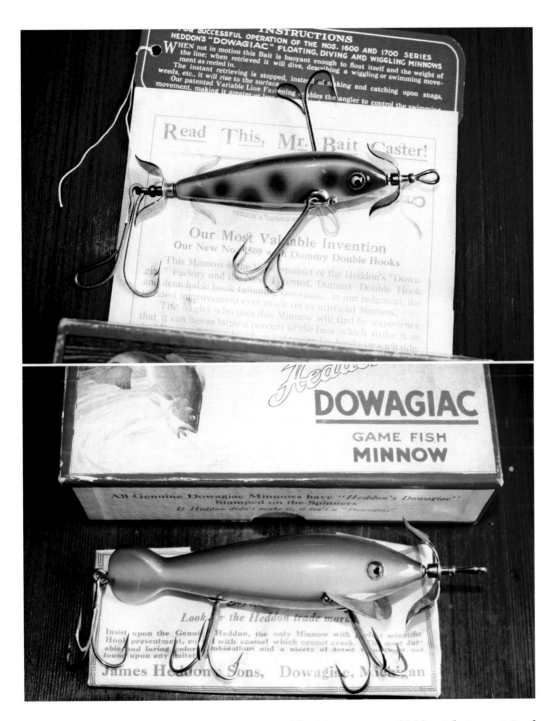

On top is a Heddon #1500 Dummy-Double Minnow ca. 1913 with its original patented hooks in Strawberry Spot color. The bottom shows the classic Heddon #3000 Spindiver in Rainbow.

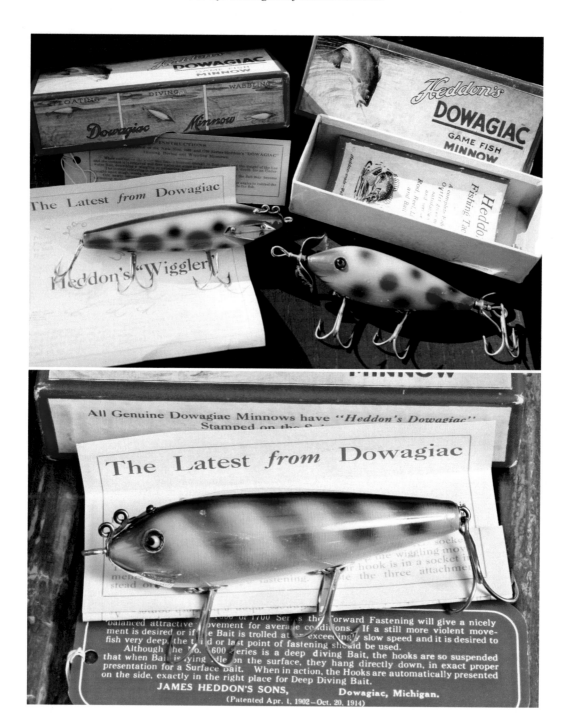

A Heddon #1600 Deep Dive Wiggler and #300 Surface Minnow, both of them in Strawberry Spot finish (ca. 1915), and a #1700 Near Surface Wiggler in Bar Perch color and "inch worm" line tie which allowed for fishing it at various depths (ca. 1914).

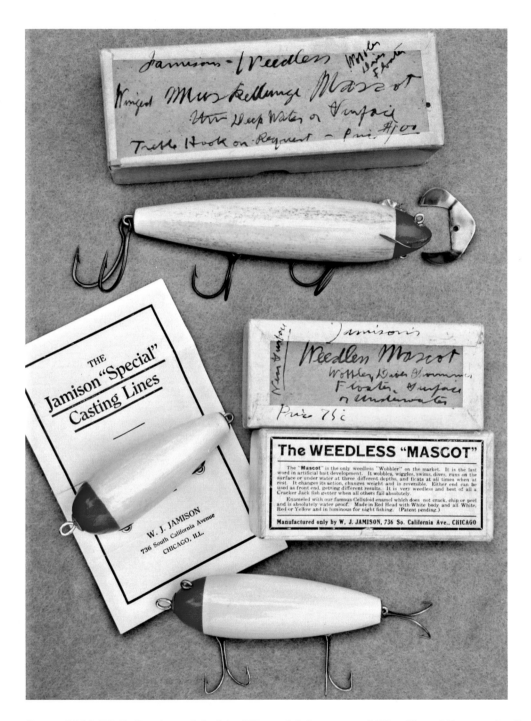

Rare 1918 W.J. Jamison Muskie Winged Mascot and Weedless Mascots in first boxes with hand-written notes from the Jamison factory.

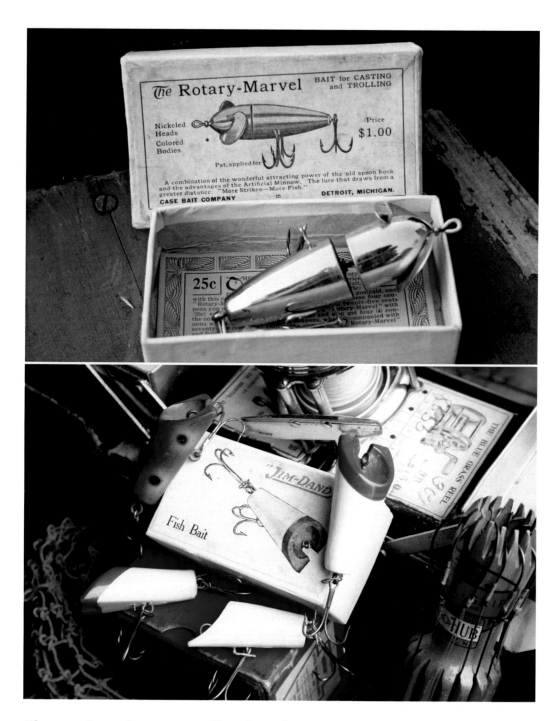

The top photo shows a rare Case Bait Co. Rotary Marvel, a nickel plated lure with a revolving head ca. 1910. On the bottom is collection of Jim Dandy wobblers ca. 1915 from Wise Sporstman's Supply Co. of Chicago, Illinois. Note the unique twisted wire hook guards.

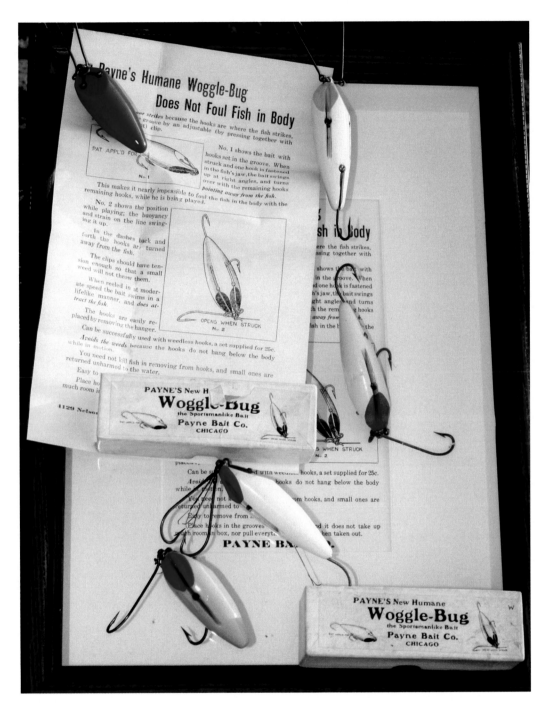

Sheridan Jones' collection of Payne's "New Human Woggle-Bug" from 1915. These lures feature three hooks, two snap into metals clips that are in wooden slots and one is stationary. The purpose of the design is to make catch-and-release easier.

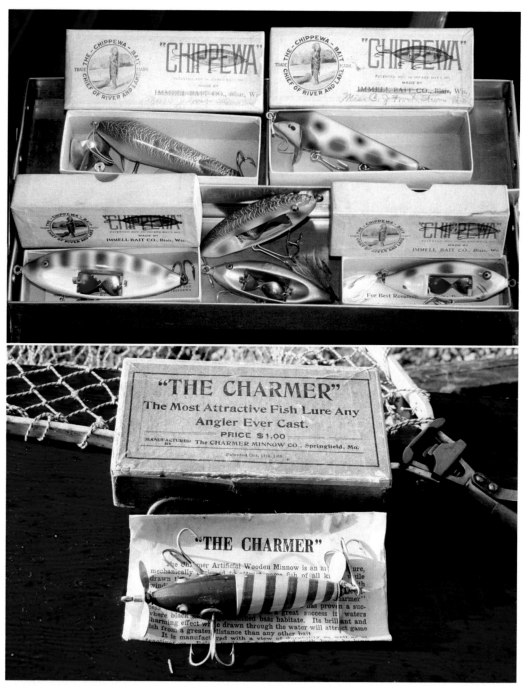

On the top is Sheridan Jones' collection of Chippewa lures. The top two lures are Chippewa Skippers with metal diving planes, the bottom four are Immel Chippewa lures in three sizes, Musky (right), Pike (Center top), and Bass (Center Bottom and Left). Bottom is an ultra rare Charmer Minnow, a barber pole bait, with German silver propellers, glass eyes, and wire-thru construction ca. 1910.

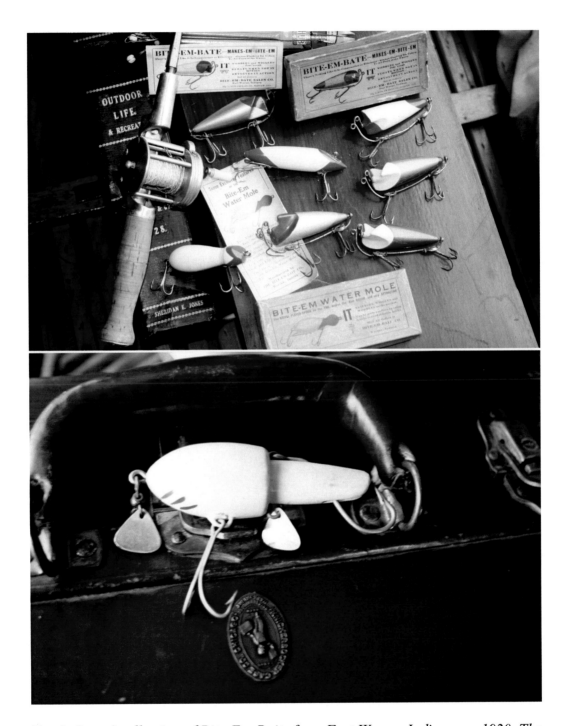

Top is Jones' collection of Bite-Em-Baits from Fort Wayne, Indiana ca. 1920. The bottom shows a rare Jim Donaly Red Fin Weedless Bait ca. 1914.

One of the greatest lures in the Sheridan R. Jones Lure Collection is this unbelievably rare James L. Donaly "Redfin" Minnow in picture box with paperwork. This classic lure from 1911 features glass eyes, hand painted gill marks, a trio of metal fins, and a hand-painted finish. A truly classic lure.

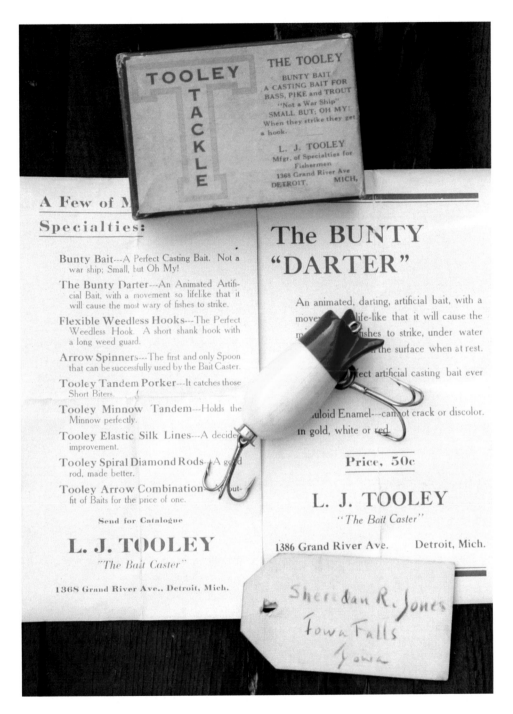

This is a rare Tooley Bunty "Darter" bait with box and paperwork ca. 1913. Tooley was a champion tournament caster, hence "The Bait Caster" nickname.

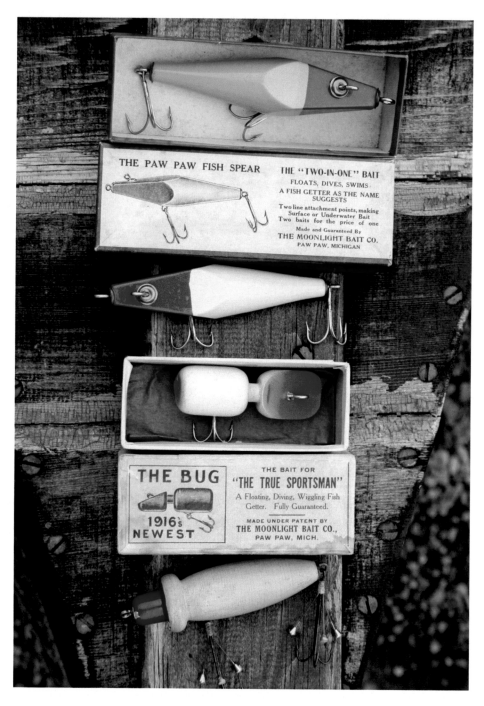

Sheridan's collection of Moonlight lures, including a pair of Fish Spear lures with double line ties advertised in 1914 as "The Two-in-One" bait. The middle lure is a Moonlight "Bug" made for "True Sportsmen" ca. 1916. At bottom is a Moonlight Weedless Floating Bait #2 ca. 1920.

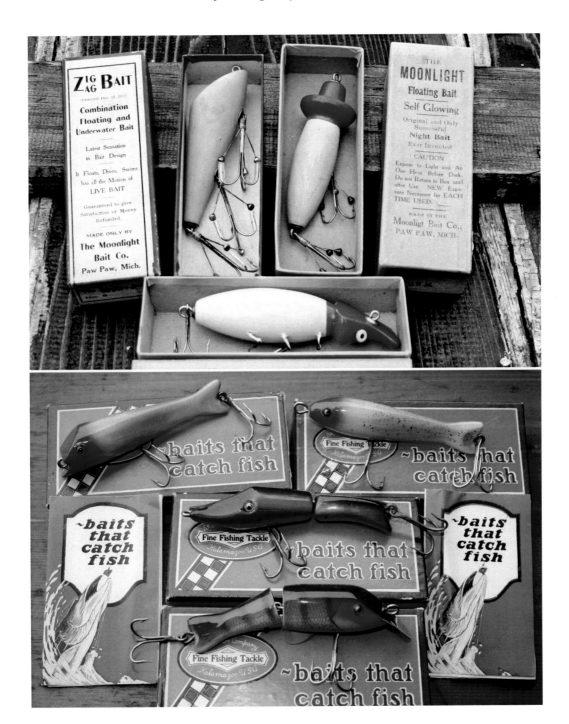

Top photo shows Sheridan's Moonlight Favorites—the Zig Wag (1914), Floating Bait Weedless (1920), and Lady Bug Wiggler (1917). Bottom is a collection of beautiful Shakespeare lures: Plopper (Top Left); Sea Witch (Top Right); Darting Shrimp (Middle Center); and Tantalizer (Bottom Center) in photo finish.

The introduction of plastic lures like the Heddon "Spook" line ca. 1930 marked a dramatic technological change in fishing history. Many of the lures pictured previously lost market share, were discontinued, or redesigned in plastic.

APPENDIX A: THE SPORT OF FISHING

ON AN ANGLING CHORD OR A TWISTED STRING?

BY SHERIDAN R. JONES

ANGLING EDITOR "OUTERS' RECREATION"

Originally published in THE OUTLOOK, *09 June 1920*

THE shores of a little Northern lake merged into that semi-darkness which precedes the arrival of a moonless night. Naught save a skyline of giant fir and balsam, appearing sinister and in profile against a rose-blue west, formed background for the ghostly close-in birch and the white crests of ripples gently lapping the sandy beach. It was the end of a day.

From out the quiet of this all-but-night floated the mellow gurgle of a paddle eagerly applied, and in from the darkness drifted the shadowy outline of a canoe feeling its way to rest at our very feet, yet yielding gracefully to the rise and fall of its own created swell. For a moment its lone occupant rested his blade, then, with the poise of one whose craft responds to every beck and call of a master, stepped upon the beach and greeted us with friendly voice. An angler returned from a day upon the lake.

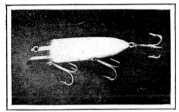

"SOME WAY THOSE HOOKS SHUT OUT THE SUNLIGHT OF 'THAT DAY'"

To complete the tale in a way that would be most satisfactory to the general pleasure-seeker there should follow the lifting of a string—a twisted string—well laden with rewards of a taking fly. Truth forbids.

"What luck, brother?"

"Great!" was his reply, and he rubbed his paddle-cramped hands in all but glee. "Great! Knew that I would get him in time. And, say, you should have seen him hit it. Met it in the air, too! Been after him for about a week; ever since I lost him when he threw a White Miller. Saw him smash at an old green dragon-fly that used to rest on the stump where he was hanging out. That gave me the big idea. Made one myself and, by Jove, I got him for sure!"

"Well, let's see him. Must be a dandy. Got him in the canoe?"

"About four pounds, I think. But he isn't in the canoe. I put him back."

"Father Isaac, man! Work a week to get such a bass, and then put him back! What in the world do you fish for, anyway?"

"Well, the fact is, I didn't have any use for him dead, and I might get another round the next time I come up. Slipped the hook from his mouth without lifting him out of the water, so I guess he was more fagged [tired] than injured. Ought to be in great shape in a day or two, after he gets his fight back."

"Yes; but what fun is there in that kind of fishing?"

"Fun? Pleasure? Didn't I catch him? Didn't I catch him on a fly? Didn't I catch him on a fly that I figured out to get him, and on one that I created myself? Fun? Pleasure? What more do you want?"

Beaching his canoe, be left us. And as his broad shoulders disappeared among the shadows above the boathouse by common consent *an angler* had returned from a day upon the lake! An angler, with his fish upon an angling chord.

All this night be a fable—an angling fable with a moral—to be read, appreciated, and forgotten. A beautiful vision, but scarcely realistic. Yet we were fortunate—fortunate in that it was a real vision, and that it came to us early in our angling career. Because of it we have turned angler rather than remained mere fisherman. Because of it we have been able to place our finest fish upon the angling chord of memory and not upon a cord of twisted string!

It is vacation time again—the play-day of a year. Throughout the length and breadth of yesterday our dreams were born and nurtured, and now in part are soon to be fulfilled. Dreams of yesteryear, of quiet cove and mighty battle; of fern-fringed book and ichthyic lore. Dreams of today, of watered vale and wooded hillock; of zephyr wand and cunning feather. We go to play.

We sort the tackle in anticipation, yet somewhere something is amiss. Perchance it is that lure—nine points it carries—a gruesome spectacle to behold! Battle-scarred and metal-tarnished, it gives mute evidence of confidence supreme. We wonder that it does not foster cherished memories, since it has served us well. But no. Some way those hooks shut out the sunlight, dim the brightness of "that day." They tell naught of balsam breezes, of singing birds and rippled waters. Their story is one of strife; their memory—a *coup de gráce*. And we were to play.

The more we angle, the more we are convinced that the spirit of fair play is essential to the gaining of recreation's pleasures and rewards. Perhaps the multiplicity of points and the assurance of staying qualities were necessary to lure men from a workaday world to the quiet places in God's great out-of-doors. If so, they have done their part and done it nobly. But one does not angle long before a new philosophy of life is born within. A square deal and a fighting chance seem all-important, while the tackle kit evolves through steady stages to a plane compatible with the spirit and purpose of the new angler.

Finesse of cast and delicacy of line control, too, have their reward in pleasure, and the victory of a taut line with no restraining barb is a "consummation devoutly to be wished." We, too, have experienced the pleasures of a day upon virgin waters, and the joy that comes to the soul as the angler gazes upon a vanquished beauty now paneled in fighting mien. We, too, have dipped our blade into the shadows of dark waters and found pleasure in the

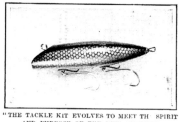

"THE TACKLE KIT EVOLVES TO MEET TH SPIRIT AND PURPOSE OF THE NEW ANGLER"

sputtering night lure and the splash of feeding bass. But never did we know the thrill of angling in all its fullness until we placed our first big, battling bronze-back upon the angling chord of memory and not upon a cord of twisted string.

The spirit of fair play has initiated am age of conservation. We doubt if the angler, deprived of his appreciation of nature's games, could be won so unreservedly to the support of a more self-producing measure. It is to the angler who loves play that we must look to carry on; it is this angler who must lead the movement of reclamation.

One of the most fruitful sources of conservation may be found in the stoppage of nature's wastes. It took long years to convince the public that such a waste was possible and that human intellect was needed to guide and direct natural processes to an advantageous conclusion. The hatchery has been one proof. Nature, tuned to an equilibrium, cannot hold her own in the face of man's destructive necessity and extravagance.

The drying of ox-bow cut-offs along our rivers in periods of low water takes a heavy toll of spring-spawned fingerling, for it is to these shallows that river fish resort for the procreative

" AN ADJACENT SLOUGH YIELDED ITS PRECIOUS QUOTA "

duties which perpetuate their kind. State and Federal Commissions have for years been saving many of these future game fish and have distributed them over wide areas. But here and there throughout the game-fish regions are hundreds, yes thousands, of such waters which commissions cannot reach or which are too small to warrant salvage of so extensive a character. This is an opportunity for local sportsmen's clubs and individuals to function in the great movement of reclamation.

We recall a chance meeting, in an out-of-the-way Mid-Western county, with two such sportsmen. True, they were clad in the simple garb of rural folk and were not of the "club" variety; but their eagerness bespoke membership in the clan of angling nobility. That they were seeking bait minnows we had no doubt, but investigation proved our error; they were reclaiming fry from a cut-off—fish that would otherwise be killed in the winter freeze.

Though angling bent, we followed the impulse of the moment and tarried to witness and finally to assist in the process till, when finally an adjacent slough had yielded to the stream its precious quota, gray shadows proclaimed the coming of night.

Yes, we lost our fishing for the day, but gained that which was better far—the joy of comradeship with nature, of knowing that we had played some part, however small, in the maintenance of a fruitful stream.

Such opportunities are open on every band, opportunities of more than passing merit. Well may the angler refine his tackle and give his support to the gospel of the taut line. Well may he join the growing brotherhood of men who "put them back" and string a needless catch upon the angling chord of memory.

But more. Join in a protest against all forces that would claim the birthright of anglers yet unborn, and stand as firmly against the "limit angler" as the illegal. Lend a strong right arm in the saving of landlocked fry and fingerling as well as in the stocking of depleted waters. And, mayhap, when the shores of that little Northern lake again take form from the semi-darkness which precedes the arrival of a summer's morn, and on the skyline the giant fir and the balsam appear in profile against a rose-blue east, 'twill be the dawn of another day—a day when men go forth *to angle*, rather than *to fish*.

That Clay-Bank Bass

The Memory of an Old-Timer.

By SHERIDAN R. JONES.

WITH ILLUSTRATION FROM PHOTOGRAPH BY AUTHOR.

Originally published in OUTER'S BOOK, *January 1915*

CLAY-BANK pool, nestling in between a fringe of maple and jack oak, lies at the foot of a high bluff of blue and yellow clay which has been partially exposed by miniature land slides. The pool itself is cut from a layer of faulted limestone and the rocky bottom at this point furnishes a playground for numerous small mouth bass, many of whom have battled their way through several seasons and are wise to the ways of the stream angler. In this pool lived an old-timer, a veteran of many battles, whose special retreat was beneath a large rock which nature had chiseled to knife-like keenness. I say *lived* somewhat joyously, for while he has skillfully eluded the net these many years, it was my good fortune to beat him on his own grounds—yet 'twas bravery that caused his downfall rather than any special cunning on the part of the angler.

Several times during the season I had drawn him from beneath that rock to inspect some new offering. On as many occasions he turned tail and retreated to his stronghold. Only once did he offer to fight like a man and savagely struck an ibis and white afast to a small gold spoon. Even here his rage overcame his sportsmanship for with a strong rush to his rocky retreat the line parted as it met the sharp edges of the monarch's home. After that he refused to notice the choicest lures that brain could devise and I had given up in despair, thinking that some more fortunate brother had turned the trick.

One afternoon, late in September, I chanced to pass this pool while seeking filling for the pan, and resolved to have one more try at that clay-bank bass. I was using a Dowagiac rainbow—the best plug for stream work on the market—and had already taken a few nice bass. But it wouldn't work on the old-timer. He knew that plug of old, had been raised with the Dowagiac family, and knew them all for traitors. It was time to do some thinking. Thinking! Wasn't I about thought out? But there had been a recent shower and the water was somewhat clouded. No doubt many

"CLAY-BANK POOL, CUT FROM A LATER OF FAULTED LIMESTONE"

choice earthworms had been washed down the slides—I would try at least. It was only the work of a moment to dig a handful of these dainties from the leaf mold beneath the trees. As I returned to the stream I sat down upon a friendly boulder and began to adjust a lively "hackle" to a small bass hook, intending to let it drift down past the well known retreat. Then some idle fancy got the better of my reason. Shifting to a No. 2-0 Carlisle, I looped the whole handful of wriggling worms upon the hook and snapped them on behind a small spinner. What a mess to look upon! Enough to send the cold chills creeping and frighten even the most self-esteemed.

Something, was it recklessness, forced me to make the cast with careless indifference to preconceived ideas of proper form, yet the lure dropped easily just beyond the rock and I started the return. Wham!! Did the rock explode? For a moment I stood gasping at the spray as it settled upon the surface, then from force of habit set the book. What happened next I scarcely remember. I see the line cut the water toward the rock. I feel the heart-sickness as thoughts of sharp-edged rock and freed captive return. Then in desperation I drop the tip and *give him slack!* Shades of Walton, what a way to fish! For a moment I stand gazing at the rock, noting the slack, and yet afraid to test it taut. Gradually my courage returns and I put a gentle strain upon the line, expecting it to give, but it is tight! Setting myself for the worst I snubbed him again with a slight motion of the tip.

Rage must have filled his old heart as he felt that sharp point pursuing him into his safe retreat, for with a vicious dash he took the deeper water, while I charged down the bank to force the fight well away from that pile of rock. And you should have seen the battle, fought as only a monarch of the pool can fight. How that little split bamboo, Jim Heddon's Favorite, responded to his vicious runs and fibre-trying plunges. Several times I thought the end had come as the current took a hand in the battle and the slender tip bent warningly. As many times it sprang back cleanly with that calm uniform tension which characterizes a splendid tool. Several times the battler cleared the water seeking for slack line, but the fighting spirit was in me and we gave no quarter. I'll admit he didn't have a square deal, for the line was new and the temptation to give the butt when he started for the rocks was greater than the thought of sportsmanship. At last he gave up.

I've been thinking the matter over since then and the taking has lost somewhat of its charm. Perhaps I shall never fish that pool again without a tinge of shame. Someway 'twould be better had I lost the battle or at least been man enough to give the freedom that so gallant a fight deserved. And why?

Years of experience had taught him to shun the spoon, to refuse the ganged minnow, to feed upon the soft-shells found beneath the rocks and nut those dangling from silken lines. And yet, here came a spinning foeman gathering up all the earthworms in the pool—wouldn't *you* fight, brother? Something tells me that he did the square thing in defending that pool from the plunderer, that the smaller bass might have plenty. Of course, they tell us there is no reason in the action of these lesser creatures; perhaps not. It may be just an idle fancy, a product of imagination, an angler's dream. And yet I feel 'twould have been better had *he* won.

One who follows the stream with rod and lure soon gets to dreaming. The very trail talks with the wilderness lover, the birds greet him joyously as he passes, the furred creatures are his friends, the spirit of the wildwood is upon him guiding his thoughts, perhaps by fancy's route, into lines which make for better, stronger, nobler living. Such dreaming pays—pays in strength of mind, of limb, of character; and let him become a wilderness dreamer who would follow the trail of life.

What did be weigh? Oh, yes, he *was* heavy, but I have no heart to remember. Some things are better forgotten. Soon I shall follow the winding path that leads toward the river, for it is fishing time again. Perchance I shall cast beside the pile of rugged rocks. But there'll be a shadow on the pool beside the jack oak, a little of the pleasure unsupplied, for there's a longing for an old companion, 'tis the memory of that clay-bank bass.

APPENDIX B: FISHING STRATEGY & TECHNIQUES

THE WITCHERY OF THE NIGHT-LINE

SHERIDAN R. JONES

Originally published in OUTDOOR LIFE, *April 1914*

EVER fish the night-line? You know its charm if you've been there; if not, what a world of mystery awaits your first trial, what alluring pleasures will crowd round you from the shadows of the shore-line. Fancy alone can picture the weird and fantastic forms that greet the night angler as he silently slips out into the darkness of a new and unknown world. Think you know the river or the favorite lake; can name each rock and mark each grassy cove and bunch of pads? You'd better think it over, brother, for they get away. Some way, somehow, they steal away into the mysterious beyond and lose themselves in the shadows of the night. It's a new world, a new river, a new lake that greets your initial effort to wet the night line, brother, and yet the pleasure of it!

It came to us by chance. We had fished through the evening hours with but little success and were drifting, listening to awakening night life in the woodland. Occasionally the clear-toned 'poor-will called to his mate. From the depths of the timber came the quivering cry of the screech-owl and the mellow voice of his larger brother. Away in the distance sounded the wail of some solitary wolf and the answering challenge of the farmer's dog. The song of many insects came to us from the reed-lined shore or sounded close at hand as some venturesome beetle winged his way across the lake. Aside from this evening chorus, quiet was abroad upon the waters. Suddenly the water broke but a few yards from the boat and almost at the same time a splash announced that some monarch of the depths had been roused from his daytime sleep to gather a

few choice insects for the evening meal. Again, near the shore, another splash; then, here and there, still others joined the sport. Could it be that these were bass? Why not try with that white surface plug? More for the sport of the thing than with any hope of success the cast was made and the return started. Bang! Had a shell exploded in

"WHEN THE NIGHT IS NOT TOO DARK"

our vicinity I doubt if we would have been more surprised. We were fast to something that lived, moved and seemed to have a being; but what it was, where it was or where it intended to go was quite another matter.

Now it takes a pretty good fighter in daylight hours to get the scribe excited, but this was something decidedly different. Excited doesn't half do justice to our, state of mind as we endeavored to play this demon of the darkness. Excited? Well I should say yes! When you haven't the slightest idea where the fish is or what he is trying to do, only feel the tip bob, bob, bob, and yank, yank, yank and hear the reel screech as he takes out line, who wouldn't get excited! After what seemed to be an hour of give and take in the darkness we had him rolling on the surface beside the boat and after two or three unsuccessful attempts to slip the net under something we at last succeeded and a lighted match revealed a two-pound bass. Two pounds! And I would have bet a hundred that he weighed at least ten!

Well, right there we decided to make an evening of it, supper or no supper. After them we went with the white Dowagiac and a well-battered Coaxer; and what a time we had. Perhaps we would be casting and fighting yet were it not for the fact that we became worse than amateurs and succeeded admirably in getting so thoroughly snarled up that it was necessary to pull for home and leave the best fishing for large-mouthed bass that has ever fallen to our lot. Oh, yes, we had a few of them, six, I believe, and one tipped the scale at six and a half. And it all happened in less than two hours with fully half that time engaged with sundry birds' nests and choked reels. Ever try to straighten out a backlash in the dark, brother? Take my advice if you value the pureness of your vocabulary, and don't. The words will come—they'll come even though you know them by sight only. Yet with it all, both pleasure and grief, we count it one of our red letter nights, for there we learned to wet the night-line!

Equipment for taking black bass at night does not differ essentially from that used during the day; yet it is wise to choose a trifle heavier tackle for obvious reasons. You will not handle your fish as skillfully as by day, with the resulting strain on both rod and line. And then, too, you'll need all the assistance a little extra weight and a trifle higher breaking strength will give you, for you will lose many a fine fish as it is. Strange, isn't it, how much one depends upon the eye in playing a fish? Personally I never thought about it until I tried casting at night. One can learn a little of the game by making a few casts with the eyes closed, at least enough to discover that it is not all plain sailing.

The rod question is easily settled—the steel by all odds is the favorite. The way it measures up in this style of angling is a pleasure to the fisherman's heart, for he knows it is a tool that will take abuse meekly and come back strong at the next east. Here is the chance for the expert to laugh and extol the merits of the split stick, but my little five-foot Bristol has witnessed that same smile disappear when the bamboo came to grief in trying to make a double turn around an oar that some way appeared in the darkness as the bass shot under the boat for deeper water. No, my friend, not the bamboo here unless you court disaster.

In matters of the reel we have a wider field, for our choice. The writer pins his faith to the South Bend anti- backlash, though perhaps another might prefer one of the other models of the self-thumbing or self-spooling habit. The choice was made because the anti- backlash comes nearest to the regular reel, causing the angler to do the major part of the work and yet freeing him from the danger that arises in not being able to watch the speed of the lure. It is an ideal night reel and there is no doubt about it. Regular reels are fickle instruments in the darkness, regular breeders of profanity, yet they can be made to answer the purpose if no other type is available. The line should be the same as for day fishing, though perhaps of slightly higher breaking strength. Any good silk will do the work but should be discarded as soon as it begins to develop weak spots.

And now the lures. A surface bait, surely. It matters not whether it be the Dowagiac, Coaxer, Red Head, Surface Charmer, White Decker or other white or light colored creation. A luminous plug such as the Moonlight or L. Coaxer is especially indicated when the night is pitch dark and the water clouded, but is not necessary in clear water under average conditions. These lures are all fish getters, yet if the water abounds in rushes and water grass, you had better tie up to Jamison's Coaxer, the one best bet in weedless night plugs. I stand ready to prove at any time and at any place that, given one bunch of grass on a ten acre cove, I can snag it three times out of four with the ordinary two or three-gang surface lure. This offer is open to all comers, the only condition being, that the fishing be done at night. One should remember also that it is not well to retrieve the lure as rapidly as by day since it seems more difficult for the fish to judge distance accurately in the darkness. When the night is not too dark, some measure of success may be had by surface fishing with live bait. Large shiners and frogs are often good fish takers and have been used with good results by many anglers yet the writer prefers the wooden plug and is convinced that it can not be surpassed as a surface lure for night fishing.

FANCY ALONE CAN PICTURE THIS "HOLE"—AT NIGHT.

But we need not give all our attention to the black bass. Most of our readers know where there is a good catfish "hole." Now a catfish of reasonable maturity is a rather stiff proposition on the night-line, and is not surpassed as a morning's bracer for the business of the day. And then sometimes we do not care to make the effort that bass fishing demands; would rather take our ease with the pole in the boat clamp and commune with the old pipe or just lazy away a few of the night hours. Let me recommend night fishing for cats—it's great! This type of fishing demands good company, real companionship, to make it most successful. There will be plenty of spare time to talk and refill the briar, plenty of time for the spinning of yarns and the pursuit of the ever present "prober." How will we do it! Just this wise:

I know of no better lure for cats than the dead minnow. An old...friend—a chronic sufferer from this disease—insists that the bait must be caught between 11 and 12 in the morning, allowed to stand in a small amount of water in the sun until evening and then be packed in damp grass until fishing time demands its removal. Whether there is any special charm in this procedure I do not know, but I do know—it catches the fish. By this treatment the bait becomes rather soft but seems to be all the more acceptable to his majesty, the cat. In fact, he has a rather perverted taste on the whole, choosing such delicacies as strong cheese, liver, chicken innards and other highly-scented bits of food, as any follower of the net or trot-line will tell you if you can get "next" to his game. But for night fishing with the bait or casting rod, a minnow (live, dead or soft), or skinned frog is surely attractive.

The hook does not need to be of the gigantic size used in connection with the trot-line, for we do not intend to stake our fish out for the night; in fact, a good bass hook is about right; it will stand all the strain that the line will take, anyway. A snelled pattern is of value, for the hook can then be threaded through the mouth, out at the gill and the point thrust through the body a trifle back of the dorsal fin. The sinker should be placed, not at the end of the line, but about ten inches, above the lure. With this rig the minnow will float just off the bottom, headed up stream, and keep in constant motion though not swinging enough to appear too active.

What a pleasure it is to sit in the darkness with the thumb resting lightly upon a free reel and feel the spool give a few inches of line; then a few more, then a few light jerks, lengthening out into an even, steady pull, the signal to set the barb. With a quick wrist movement the hook takes firm hold in what seems to be a sunken log. Oh, yes, but is it! Well, hardly! You will have a fight, brother, and fight is the word! Ever cut out a five pounder? You've got to give it to him; he'll put up the liveliest scrap that you will care to handle—in the dark, mind you. Then when you slip the net under him, just picture to yourself a plate' stacked full of catfish steak fried to a turn and browned in butter, with its accompaniment of flapjacks and coffee! Is there many a dish or many a fish that is its equal?

Where's another good night-line fish that should not pass unnoticed. Know a "gang" of boys in your neighborhood that need looking after! It's a good plan to be in on the nightly "doings" of said boys, good for your peace of mind and your movable October property, and, also good for the boys if you meet them half way. How about taking a bunch of them down to the river after dark and fishing for bull-pout? Yes, take the "eats" along, and an extra large frying pan.

'NOUGH SAID—BULL POUT 'N EEL.

Build a huge bonfire on the bank and get them all busy with the "Yellow bellies" while you start the spuds a-roasting and fill the coffee can. About the first thing you know some lad will connect up with an eel and then your hands will be full, for of course the said eel must go into the pan. Like as not you will be the only one who "dares" skin him. Don't shirk now, for did you, not tell 'em how fine fried eel used to taste when you were a boy? Now, a boy hates a quitter; stick it out at all hazard. Soon there are more than enough fish for the pan, and while a few of the lads are cleaning the catch, the rest will be busily engaged with a few extras to take home to the folks.

Ever see boys eat? Ever eat like a boy yourself? You will grow years younger for such a night. You will feel more like a man, for you have given that pleasure which would have been priceless to your boyish heart. And you will have a "gang" that will guard you and yours far better than any hand that commands by fear and force. Try it once, brother, and you'll go again.

There are, perhaps, three types of night anglers: One wedded to the sport because business precludes the enjoyment of many daylight trips; a second comes from shady nooks after the hot hours of the midsummer day have been spent, to take up the night-line as a lesser evil; the third shoves his boat out into the darkness because he is a dreamer, a disciple of Nature, a lover of the great outdoors. To him no day is complete when darkness fails to contribute its quota of Nature secrets; no joy as sweet as that which comes from trying the untried. Yet perhaps there is a fourth—the angler who has never thought much about it; would have tried, only never seemed to go; couldn't get anyone to go and play the fool game with him, and a score of other reasons for his natural timidity. Come! Let it be tonight! Nay delay the start when a start is all you need? You have never half realized what it means to really know a river or a lake; you can never half appreciate the thrill of the savage strike and the glorious uncertainty of that first rush for freedom, until you have drifted away into the darkness, following the Red God's call—the witchery of the night-line.

Black Bass and Basscraft

Chapter XI—The Small-mouth of the Pools

By SHERIDAN R. JONES

Originally published in OUTER'S RECREATION, *July 1920.*

THERE are, of course, stream fishermen galore—but the number of anglers who really know how to fish all the water of a stream and net bass from all possible locations is far below what it should be, to say the least. Perhaps the greatest factor contributing to this result is to be found in the fact that the vast majority never pass the primary grades in angling-craft.

They have learned to take bass by having mastered one or two situations; this is sufficient. More seems neither essential nor to be desired.

Ye scribe early discovered that there was more to bass angling than the taking of a few fish. There was in our neighborhood an angler who seemed to possess more than ordinary wisdom.

It was a common saying that this fellow could catch bass in a roadside pool, so regularly did he turn the trick. Fair weather or foul, rain, sun or storm, the trip that netted not a few for this angler's pan was a rarity. We put it down to luck, at first, but the more we thought about it the more we were convinced that selling insurance and catching fish might be worked out along the same lines—he studied men, and made good; why should not a like understanding bring equal results in the game of angling? We never wrested the secret of his success from his own lips, but we have had the courage of our own convictions and are now convinced that we have found the real reason—he knew men, and again, he knew bass. The master-craftsman learns not his trade in a day.

To the average fisherman of the streams a pool is the prime invitation to wet a line and, because of its many possibilities, is usually the most fruitful location for the unskilled. There are certain seasons and again certain places and times when the pool is not good weather for smallmouth. That is, a pool in the general sense of the term. However, since bass frequent such areas for several reasons throughout the day and year, it is well to find out when and where a well placed lure is apt to connect. There are certain pool possibilities—let us take them up in order.

There is first of all the deep pool with little or no bottom hiding, few and small shoreline rock areas, and practically no white-water at its head. Rather uninviting, but sought by bass during the heat of the day in mid-summer or when the water lowers, driving them from other favorite spots. Add to the picture clear water and bright sunshine, and the angler has his work cut out for him if he is to succeed.

Bass in such a location are not feeding, are not aggressive nor again pugnacious. They are keen to appreciate a careless shadow, suspicious beyond degree, and usually safe. However, just at dusk and for some time thereafter, these same fellows will work up toward the head of the pool or out toward the shoreline in search of supper, a meal which must last them throughout the coming day. It has been our experience that this is the greatest opportunity ever offered the fly-man to pass out a sample of his wares with some degree of success. A well placed fly will prove the downfall of many such bass, and we like a floater along the edges of the stream with the wet fly running stronger just at the edge of the rapids. The pattern does not seem to matter but the size plays a very important role—sometimes large and again small, as the passing whims of the quarry may dictate. We have not found that the light colored offerings are any better than the dull

The wet fly runs strong just at the edge of the rapids.

patterns, though we do prefer a touch of tinsel in the make-up of the fly. Perhaps a bit of the sparkle remains in the half light that is attractive.

It is next to impossible to pick up these fellows during the hours of daylight unless the pool is approached and fished without the angler showing his person or shadow to the resting fish. However, a big, red earthworm looped easily on a single hook will take them if it is allowed to float down with the current into the middle of the pool. The fly rod is, of course, indicated and the leader, of six foot length, should be invisible (mist or water color). Having taken one fish, rest the pool for an hour or two; no need to try again until things settle down a bit. We like to tie a small twig or bit of bark to the leader, just enough to keep the worm off the bottom, if the current is too slow to move the leader alone. Watching this tiny "bobber," lying flat on your belly beside the pool, is neck breaking work—but it sure gets the bass. If you are a trout fisherman you will at once appreciate the method; if not, try it and be convinced that fishing a clear pool requires craftsmanship of the highest sort.

Another pool possibility is to be found usually in the more rapid streams. This is one with probably less depth than the first mentioned but rock and boulder strewn along its deepest parts. For genuine A-1 pool smallmouth fishing we commend the rock-bottomed deep-water to your attention. The surface will be smooth and uninviting, but down in the depths, lying behind their rocky break-waters, are the choicest bronzebacks of the stream.

These fish seem to be in an entirely different mood from the denizens of the clear pool. They are hidden fish, and a hidden bass will always take a chance. Not if you make a big fuss about it and herald your presence in either form or shadow, but to the careful angler they strike with regularity. Their food comes to them with the current, sometimes swinging into the deadwater should the rock be large, but more frequently dashing past in its journey down current. They take it with an energy and a speed that permits but little pre-consideration, and we prefer a fast lure for this reason. The most deadly offering ever invented for this situation; is a big bunch of red worms, floated down past the rock hidings in the late afternoon. In fact, it is so taking that it ceases to be a sporting proposition and borders closely upon the pleasure of worming for sunnies on the mid-depth bars. For this reason, because the black bass of the fast water streams merits a fighting chance, because a mess and more is not the sole satisfaction in angling, for this reason we have come to discard the humble worm when the quarry lies behind the rocks and feeds with malice toward none and forethought not at all. Give him at least a fighting chance!

The most sportive proposition for this situation is the fly rod and small spinner, or, should you be a trifle more at home in the fly fishing game, the fly fished wet, yes, very wet. A small, slim, gold or brass spoon with a Colonial Fuller fly, preferably in tandem, is our first choice in spinners. On the streams regularly fished by us it is the most killing proposition of its kind. When this fails we often try a nickel or aluminum blade and a Lake George, Parmachene Belle or Split Ibis. Getting no response to this offering, we go after the "Killer." What is this? Just a little fancy of our own that sure brings home the bacon. Behind a very small round blade we hang a long shanked hook. Just below the eye of the hook is tied a stubby shackle of bucktail (red or yellow), the strands not over one-half inch in length and the hook extending out behind for probably three-fourths inch. Placing on the hook a small sliver of pork rind we are ready to take up the fly rod and band out good medicine. Does it work? Well, you try it when smallmouth hide behind the rocks, and see for yourself.

The expert flyman will here find opportunity to try out his fancies but, because we shall have a chapter devoted entirely to the fly fishing game, we pass the matter by with but the suggestion. We would recommend, however, that your pattern be fished submerged unless it is a typical dry fly stream and dry fly weather, of which more anon.

Rock-hiding, pool bass are summer and fall game. True a few may be taken during the earlier months, especially should the stream be minus good whitewater, ledge and shoreline depths, but for summer and in fact my hot weather fishing we look to the rocks to yield a goodly share. We prefer late afternoon when the sun begins to cast long shadows, though at sundown we would try other water for maximum results.

To fish such water with success requires a complete knowledge of the pool during times of low and exceptionally clear water; otherwise it will be a bit and miss affair from start to finish. We remember one time in particular that caused us a great deal of amusement. Working along our favorite stream one sunny afternoon we came upon two strangers fishing with live minnows in a certain pool. To our inquiry they reported no success and were thinking of giving it up. Knowing this particular spot very well we made the remark that we believed there was a good bass right out in front of them and, if they didn't mind our butting in, we would take it out before going further up the river. Getting a line on a certain tree standing opposite, we placed our spinner right across the nose of a big submerged boulder a few feet farther out than they bad been fishing. Scarcely had it started its erratic motion before—bang!!—we hung a pretty little two-pound small-mouth. Of course they commented upon the "luck of some dobbers," and we admitted that it did seem that way. How often since have we recalled with a smile the facial expressions of our stranger friends as they saw that little fighter leave the water time and time again. Luck? Well, perhaps.

Another mighty fine pool possibility, not regularly found in the smaller streams, is where the current cuts into a grassy bank making a miniature whirlpool with under-bank pockets. Here the deep water is at the shoreline. Usually the fisherman spoils his chances by coming right out on the bank and dropping his line into the center of the quiet area. Now, before being frightened by his approach, the bass were lying under the edge of the bank, looking for insects, a stray frog, larvae of various kinds and possibly a few worms that might happen to work out of the leaf mold in the grass, A lure placed just at the margin and retrieved out and down, being cast from below and across, is a taking method, and that it should be a fly or very small spinner and fly goes without saying. This is about the only stream situation, too, where we would recommend the grasshopper and cricket to the exclusion of other live offerings. At times they are most acceptable to bank bass, and good artificials (there are some now on the market) are about as successful as the real thing.

While in most streams bass come few and far between during the very hot weather and especially during the heat of mid-summer days, should the angler be able to locate a pool into which the water from a cold spring is flowing he will be reasonably sure of some success. The depth of the pool matters but little since the inflow is cold and it is the cooler water that our bass are seeking. It is at first surprising how close to the shoreline and in what shallow areas one will find bass at such times. We have taken two and three pounders from water that would scarcely cover their backs—this when the sun was exceptionally hot and the cool currents inshore. While we can see no reason why these fellows should be pugnacious or greedy at such times, nevertheless they will strike a spinner, especially should it be followed by a single hook well laden with worms, big, red worms. It has been our experience that they will take this more regularly than the spinner and fly and we have not often been able to get them interested in the fly alone. The hotter the weather the more apt are bass to be found in such locations.

Occasionally one will be able to locate a deep pool that is receiving water from a bottom spring. Here the bass will be lying near the spring-hole and must be angled for in much the same manner as was suggested in the case of the rock-free pool. They seem to be easily interested in the angler's careful offering, possibly because the cool water gives them a little snap and ambition. While the spinner is an exceptional offering for such fish, a live minnow will usually be well received, for the small fry also seek the cooling influence of the incoming water and the smallmouth takes toll from their numbers.

No doubt the very best pool possibility, unless it be the deep rock strewn areas, is to be found where some tributary creek enters the main stream. Just outside the bar, which usually forms at the creek's mouth, will be deeper water and it is here that the fisherman will get great sport in the evening. Evening, get it, 'tis poor day water. We never think of this situation without reaching for the fly-book, for if ever the stream angler is to rely upon the fuzzy lures it is at such a time as this. Standing a little below the incoming water and casting into its edge, permitting the fly to dance along on the surface or be partially submerged, the thrills of the light rod will be experienced. Shifting from one pattern to another, or better from twos to fours or even to sixes and eights, if you can't make them take a fly here—you might as well go back to bait fishing and be done with it. As the night shadows close in upon the shoreline your chances increase and we can not wish you better luck, brother, than to stand in such a place when the bronze-backed boys are in the mood.

We have not spoken of bait for this situation. We hesitate to profane a bit of fly-water with a dead sure proposition. It robs angling of its charm when the element of skill gives way before the desire to get fish at any cost. Of course if you must have them for the pan, play to their appetites, for these are feeding fish. Your helgramite, your softshell, worm and minnow will all suffice—in the half-light they are well nigh irresistible. But for right down sport add a bit of finesse to the angling game by dropping a fly where the waters meet. A two pound bass, won by the charm of a dancing Baltimore or Belle; a battle royal crowned with victory for the better craftsman; and bass or bacon, we'll not complain!

APPENDIX C: ANALYSIS OF FISHING LURES

Outers'- 🐟 -Recreation

Kindly address all letters of inquiry to Mr. Jones or "Editor, Angling Department." It will help to avoid delay and bring a prompt response

With Bait and Fly

Your opinion on any angling subject may be of value to others. Let us have it for their benefit

Edited by SHERIDAN R. JONES

Black as a Lure Color

By Sheridan R. Jones

Originally published in OUTER'S RECREATION, May 1916.

PRACTICALLY ever since lure fishing first began red has been considered the standard attractive color in the make-up of an artificial offering, and red has its attractive qualities in the sight of fish without question. Yet another color has been crowding red for a place in the fishing sun, during the past few years, and bids fair to become just as universally used in the pattern of a fishing lure. We have in mind black, solid black, dead black, just black and no more—and black can be considered as a color from the fisherman's point of view.

In this brief discussion of black as a lure color we do not have in mind the making of definite statements of known fact; rather would we offer a few observations made while using a black lure, in the hope that anglers generally may experiment with lures of this color, in order to determine the value of such a sombre shade in the sight of fish. We hope to hear from all who give black a thorough try out during the coming season, and especially do we desire to learn the value of black when substituted for red—both as a solid color and in the place of red in combination with white and with the other colors commonly used in lure building.

Tests with certain fish in the experimental scientific laboratory, while not conclusive, leave a reasonable doubt as to the ability of certain species to differentiate between red and black. Their behavior would indicate that a red light may be the

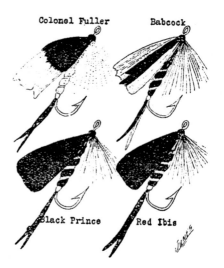

Colonel Fuller   Babcock

Black Prince   Red Ibis

same as no light at all, or at least as so little light that it is not able to produce the responses ordinarily given when the fish are in the presence of colors other than red. As suggested above, there is a reasonable assumption that fish, certain species at least, do not distinguish between red and black and that, as a result of this lack of distinction, red lures and black lures may appear to the fish as one and the same thing as far as color is concerned. We say this is a reasonable assumption and not a clearly demonstrated fact; and so we plan to give the assumption the benefit of the doubt during the coming season, hoping as well that many other anglers will make careful observations along the same line to the end that we may have considerable data upon which to base our conclusions at the close of the present fishing year.

We have been working on this "hunch," off and on during the past year or two and have noted several points that have been interesting in the extreme. In many ways our findings have been verified by those of other anglers, as evidenced by the increasing popularity of black as a standard color in the making of lures primarily designed for bass. As a trout lure color black has always been a favorite, though usually with a touch of other color in the body or in the tag.

Some of our observations have been but partially completed, yet we will offer those that furnish an opportunity for other anglers to test out the suggested possibilities. One of these is the use of the Black Prince fly on trout. Practically every trout angler well knows the taking quality of the Black Prince fly. We have often noted that this fly with the red tag would take trout when the same pattern, minus the tag, would not get a rise. Naturally our first conclusion was, in effect, that the dash of red was noted by the trout and that red was essential in the combination as red. Yet this is not necessarily a correct conclusion.

There are other possibilities. In the first place, the red in connection with the Black Prince fly is a tail tag; its absence destroys the pattern of the fly since it does away with a tag. May it not be that trout desire a Black Prince *with a tag* instead of seeking the red of the tag? Again, since all colors appear as different shades of gray to the totally color blind human eye, may it not be that the red tag appears dark gray to the fish, or some shade of gray determined by the amount of white light mixed with the red? It would be interesting to tie a few Black Prince, patterns with black, dark gray, medium and light gray tags and to fish them against a Black Prince with the red tag, when trout were taking this fly. We have not tried this on trout since our recent experimenting has been almost entirely on bass.

In the latter fish we have not discovered any difference between a Black Prince with black tag and the same pattern with the customary red tag. Using another fly as an illustration, the Colonel Fuller. We have dressed this fly with a black over-feather instead of with the red and have found it to kill right along with the regular dressing, as uniformly as our meager experimenting has been able to show. We have tied it also with a dark gray over-feather but can not report on this combination as yet with any degree of certainty. It seems, however, that the gray over-feather has a tendency to rob the fly of some of its attractive features.

We have also experimented with the Babcock, dressing it with red hackle and over-feathers, black body and half-red tag. With this dressing we have fished it as a leader fly in combination with a standard pattern dropper and have been unable to note any difference in the taking qualities of either fly. Our findings thus far may or may not mean that black is the equivalent of red in the make up of these two patterns. We desire to give more time to these experiments before reaching a definite conclusion.

Thee last set of experiments in connection with flies on bass was extremely interesting in that we fished a coal black Black Prince, one with a black tag and very black hackle, against a Red Ibis without being able to find one bit of evidence that the bass could distinguish between the two dressings! The black fly was killing just as consistently as the red. It is true that in this test we were not using the fly as a fly alone but in combination with a small spoon and trout sized rind. There is always the possibility that the bass were striking rind for rind's sake or the small spoon for the sake of the glitter. Nevertheless we worked this combination on so many waters and at such entirely different times that the results are suggestive to say the least. It will be noted from the illustrations that these two flies, the Black Prince and the Red Ibis, are practically identical in pattern if we consider red the equivalent of black as far as fish optics are concerned.

Passing now to the realm of the plug we find a similar situation in the white with red head and the white with black bead. In our experiments we used the Bass-Oreno, using one doctored up to carry a black head. The few experiments carried out seemed to indicate that when the white with red head was killing, the white with black head would kill equally well. Here, again, it may have been the white body that was the attractive feature or it may have been the pronounced action of the lure that was killing. But the results were again suggestive. Our experiments also covered the solid colors but, unfortunately, two different types of action were used because the only ones at our disposal were an all red and an all black in the same lure. Both were wobblers, however, and both drew strikes although it seemed that the solid black was the, more attractive in this case. This may have been due to the fact that it was the action of the solid black that was the more desired, or it may have indicated that the bass were distinguishing between the red and the black. The red was getting sufficient strikes, however, to make the experiment suggestive.

Looking back over our attempts to substitute black for red we are inclined to the belief that trout show a keener differentiation between lure colors than do bass. It is just possible that trout are governed in their, choice by the amount of white light mixed with the real color and that red, possessing some of this white light not present in black, appears to them as a certain shade of gray, while bass do not get it as a gray at all. This is a possibility suggested-by the fact that trout distinguish so readily between the different sombre colored flies, a fact that all trout students will readily recognize. Could we but substitute the proper shade of gray in regular highly colored trout patterns, might they not be just as taking as the gay colors? We do not know.

As we pointed out at the beginning of this article, we do not say that black and red appear the same in color value to all fish, nor even that they appear the same to any fish. We have, however, experimented enough to let a reasonable doubt enter the equation as far as bass are concerned at least. That black is one of the most, attractive colors as far as bass lures are concerned we have no doubt whatever. That it is just as attractive as red we are almost ready to believe. That it is the same to a bass as red we are not quite ready to admit, yet it would not surprise us in the least if such a conclusion were ultimately forced upon us after much experimentation with black substitutions.

In conclusion we would reiterate our suggestion that this matter be given careful consideration by anglers with an experimental turn of mind, trying black against red on bass and black or dark green against red on trout as well. It is possible, and perhaps probable, that we shall discover a real color distinction as the basis for a choice as between red and black in both feathers and solid lures. There seems to be the possibility that such a distinction, when made, is based upon the presence of white lights in red, and even the possibility of a total lack of ability to differentiate, at least in certain species of fish.

Outers'— —Recreation

Kindly address all letters of inquiry to Mr. Jones or "Editor, Angling Department." It will help to avoid delay and bring a prompt response

With Bait and Fly

Your opinion on any angling subject may be of value to others. Let us have it for their benefit

Edited by SHERIDAN R. JONES

The New "De Luxe" Scale Finish

By Sheridan R. Jones

Originally published in OUTER'S BOOK, MARCH 1915.

THE angler who is just taking up the bait-casting game and makes his initial selection of lures from the well stocked shelves of the modern tackle emporium, looks upon the present-day casting plug as a thing of beauty and a joy forever. Those of us of more mature years who have followed the casting game from its very beginning and who have seen the birth and development of hundreds of offerings (and also attended the death rites of many), realize that the present state of perfection has only been attained after long years of effort and after many, many failures.

Where is the old timer who does not remember the first hand-painted cedar blocks that posed as lures? Who does not call to mind the case with which the gangs parted from the blocks, the beautifully swollen and water-soaked plugs, their dull house paint coats and peeling enameled dressings? Who does not recall the stir a certain manufacturer caused when he put out the first enamel "guaranteed not to crack," and who does not recall as well that it did crack?

But things have changed. We now have hooks that stick until the lure is battered beyond all recognition. The celluloid enamel of most offerings is as peel-proof as could be desired and the wood is water-proofed until swelling is a negligible factor, even though the teeth of lunge and pike do penetrate. Truly the modern plug is a thing of beauty and a joy forever.

Colors and patterns galore are displayed before us and not the least of these is the good old red and white that is always found in the angler's kit. The rainbow, too, has been a standard

All with the new finish

finish, as has also the solid red. Other colors for special times and special waters, some of them doubtful in efficiency and some taking, are the solid yellow, white, black, gray, mouse white, silver, gold, luminous, colored backs with white belly, fancy spotted effects, frog, perch, crab, and black sucker. But now there comes a new one that bids fair to take a foremost place-the "de luxe" scale finish-the exact imitation of the minnow.

The writer last year had occasion to give this finish a thorough tryout and found that it was in every way a taking pattern. As a matter of fact, in the type of lure tried, it killed more bass under a greater variety of conditions than any of the other colors in which the plug mentioned is supplied. At all times the water was clear, however, and the plug was easily seen. No occasion presented itself to test it out in clouded water where, we believe, the red and white or plain white would have excelled. Still-fished in the morning, at midday and in the evening; in sunshine, in shadow, and in rain-the scale finish killed more bass. While we endeavored to make the trial as fair to all finishes as was possible, it is not necessary, to say that this new coloration is the best for bass. It will be sufficient to note that it is a most killing pattern in the lure mentioned, and we can look forward to the trials with other baits to establish real merit.

The scale finish was introduced to the anglers last season. This at least was the first plug to come to our desk that was finished along the lines that seem to be so popular this year among manufacturers. In fact, it was a very close imitation of the coloration found on the chub and as such is not surpassed by the later arrivals.

While there is considerable difference in this finish as made use of by the several plugmen, it is in truth more nearly a nature pattern than the frog, crab, black sucker, or perch, though the latter coloration is perhaps the best copy among the four mentioned. The peculiar shape and action of a plug in the water makes the copy of a food minnow more lifelike than that of the frog or crab, and the addition of the scale finish sets off the offering as really worthy of the term nature finish.

The Creek Chub was described in these columns last year so we need not have more to say about it here than that it is a first-class imitation, possessing much of the iridescent sheen of the chub, The finish as applied by the Dowagiac people shades from a silver streak upon the back, through dark to iridescent green upon the upper sides, then silver to a white belly. Head dusted with gold and rather larger scales than are found on the other baits. The Jamison offering is much the same, though does not have the silver dorsal streak and tends toward silvery sides rather than iridescent, belly white. A bright crimson band runs along the sides, head slightly gold dusted, though darker and more like the back. The scales are small and silvery. In the fourth plug finish there is a dark back tending toward brownish as it meets the gray sides, which merge into the customary white. The head is gold dusted as in the second plug and the scales, a silvery green, stand out as darker spots upon the lighter ground color. It is difficult to de- scribe the exact points of difference, though these are apparent when com- paring the baits and one could easily pick the makers if shown but a -small portion of the finish. In fact, while all mentioned above are in reality but modifications of the same idea, still each possesses an individuality all its own.

No doubt many other manufacturers will sooner or later put out their offerings in this finish and they will be presented to the readers of *Outer's Book-Recreation* as soon as possible so that a line may be had on their special dressing. However, they will, for the most part at least, probably conform to this type since putting the scale finish upon other backgrounds departs from the coloration of the bait minnow and will be of doubtful value as an exact copy.

APPENDIX D: THE SCIENCE OF FISHING

50   Outers'–  –Recreation

How Well Do Fish Hear?
By Sheridan R. Jones

Originally published in OUTER'S RECREATION, January 1922

MANY interesting discussions have appeared from time to time in connection with the question of hearing in fish. Where is the fisherman who has not often been admonished by companions to "cut out that whistling" or to stop making "that infernal racket" so as to give the fish a chance to bite? How often do we hear that Brother So and So is or ought to be a good fisherman since he never talks? How many fellows have the nerve to sing "Hail, hail, the gang's all here" while endeavoring to coax a sly old *fontinalis* to take a chance at a skillfully placed floating hopper? Where is the fisherman who does not at least have a "hunch" that fish can bear? And yet the question of hearing among fish will start a discussion pro and con in any group of anglers.

We have neither desire nor inclination to go into the scientific aspects of the matter, however interesting such investigations might be to those with sufficient scientific training to comprehend the data presented. We shall endeavor, however, to present the case in such a way as to make it plain to the every- day anglers, refraining from technical nomenclature where possible and offering explanations where scientific terms must be used, So get the old briar drawing freely and sit in while we talk this matter over with the clan.

In the first place, one of the reasons why there is so much difference of opinion among anglers when the subject of hearing is brought up, is that we are not just agreed upon

WHEN Brother Jones, in the fullness of his scientific knowledge, voices an opinion, it is entitled to respect, and in this particular case I can accept his verdict the more readily because I arrived at the same conclusion more than a quarter of a century ago, in this manner.

Because a grouchy fishing pal had upbraided me for whistling in the boat, I determined to make a little investigation to see how well fish might hear. In the walled pool at the old club house were several bass and pickerel, for whose benefit I pounded two large stones together above the water, without disturbing them in the least. Then I found two smaller stones and gently tapped them under the water. The bass jumped instantly, but the pickerel did not move. I repeated the experiment again and again, always with the same result. Striking the stones as hard as I could, I failed to disturb the pickerel but the bass were in a panic. From all of which I concluded that my grouchy Pal was needlessly alarmed about the whistling, but might have been justified in kicking about a thump on the bottom of the boat.

Which proves—if it proves anything—that there is no need of waiting for the scientist to tell you everything you may want to know about fishes.

—The Editor.

what constitutes hearing and the character of the sense organs necessary to the process, Hearing may be defined roughly as the ability to sense vibrations, and since there may be vibrations in Solids, liquids and gases, vibrations which may pro- duce hearing can be carried through the earth, the water and the air.

Scientific experiments demonstrate clearly that vibrations of the air, while violent enough to cause intense sounds sensed by an animal whose ear is constructed to pick up air vibrations, are killed when coming into contact with either liquids or solids, or so materially reduced as to be out of the question as far as the sense of hearing is concerned. Let the angler but plunge his bead under water and "listen" to his companion fire his heavy revolver or shotgun. Listen will be about as far as he will get, for there will be no report as far as he is concerned. This is but a simple way to demonstrate the truth of what may be demonstrated in a more accurate manner scientifically. Air vibrations are killed at the meeting, point of air and water.

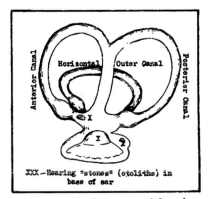

XXX.—Hearing "stones" (otoliths) in base of ear

Right ear canals of salmon viewed from the inside. These canals are imbedded in solid bone or cartilage, with no external openings.

This being true, it is impossible for a fish, no matter how keen his sense of hearing may be, to hear the air vibrations that are sounds to you and to me. Of course, exceptions must be made for such sounds as crashes of thunder and violent explosions, which are, in part only, communicated to the waters and ground in sufficient intensity to be picked up POSSIBLY by organs of hearing. We say "possibly" for we have no information that such is the case. And such violent, vibrations of the air would scarcely be classed by you and by me as being sounds within the sense of the subject under discussion. We may then safely establish the point here that air vibrations, sounds in the air, have no effect upon animals while submerged in water. Hence fish do not hear a "whistle," "an infernal racket," nor are they disturbed by a vocal selection such as "Hail, hail," etc,

However, we have not answered the question, do fish hear? in the negative. It is easily demonstrated that fish can sense vibrations produced in the water itself as well as vibrations communicated to the water from vibrating solids—such as ground, rock, wood and metal. While in man the only sense organ capable of detecting vibrations resulting in hearing is the ear (a sense organ designed to pick up vibrations of the air), in fish there are three organs which can, to a greater or less extent, pick up vibrations of the water and interpret these in terms of hearing—the ear, the lateral line, and the skin.

It is not important in this discussion to determine which of the three is the most important. Suffice it to say that all three work together to the end that a fish possesses what a scientist would term an acusticolateral system of hearing, with possible cutaneous modification or assistance—which means an ear-lateral line system with possibly, yes probably, some skin modification or assistance.

It is a matter of easy demonstration that fish respond in a definite form of behavior to vibrations either produced in the water' or in solid materials which are in direct contact with the water. Clap two stones together under water, producing thereby water vibrations, and a response-a hearing response-is the direct result. Drop a heavy rock upon the bank near a pool and note the confusion among the minnows and larger fish as a result.

We can fix, then, a second definite point in the discussion—namely, that fish are sensitive to water vibrations and to vibrations in solids which are in direct contact with water. Since sensitivity to vibrations of any kind of material substance, gas, liquid, or solid, is hearing, we cannot but conclude that fish can hear. However, their hearing is confined to vibrations produced in water or in solids and communicat6d to water, but not in air communicated to water either directly or through a solid medium.

It is well to remember also, that their bearing sense organ is a triple affair and hence very sensitive—probably more so than we at present suspect; that they become aware of many slight vibrations even though their response to them is of a passive rather than an active nature.

Summing up the possibilities, then, fish cannot hear sounds that are produced in the air—such as singing, shouting, whistling or the discharge of firearms. They can and do readily hear vibrations of the water—splashes, clapping together of stones under water, the grind of oarlocks and clumsy feet in the boat, and the tread of the angler's feet upon the bank of the pool.

The above conclusions are based upon scientific experimentation, and not upon the erratic and uncontrolled judgments of the layman angler. We do not deem it necessary nor profitable to go into the detail of the experimentation in a general article of this nature, however interesting it might be to anglers who are scientifically inclined and trained.

There are, however, several sidelights of interest developed out of the experimental data that may prove of practical value to the angler who desires to understand why all fish do not respond in the same way and to the same degree when confronted by water vibrations presented under identical conditions, We shall take up a few of these.

The degree of activity manifested by a fish on hearing a vibration is not necessarily an accurate measure of the amount of vibration sensed by said fish, since activity is only one form of behavior—we have both active and passive behavior. Just because a fish darts off in a frightened manner is no reason for supposing that he has sensed a vibration more keenly than has a second fish which makes no move at all nor responds by a mere quiver of the pectoral or caudal fins. Different species of fish show a marked difference in their response to vibrations. Some dart away quickly from the source of the vibration, some simply become alert, white others will move toward the source of the vibration in question. This is, easily demonstrated by confining several species of fish in a large container and striking the side of the container a sharp blow; or a pebble may be thrown into a pool, and a different type of behavior may be noticed among the small fish gathered there should the pool contain several species. The splash of a bait will apparently frighten some fish, but it is equally true that it will attract others.

Fish that have become accustomed to certain vibrations, such as the passing of wagons over a bridge, and will not move when such vibrations come to them, will dart away as the footfall of an angler, approaching from upstream, reaches them—coming from a different source. Or the click of a hobnail against a rock in midstream may frighten a trout that rests quietly while a wagon is being driven along a roadway bordering the stream, while his brother upstream will go into a panic at the footfall of a bank angler.

Fish of the same species will respond to similar vibrations differently, depending upon their "education." It is well for the angler to bear in mind that a fish may be attracted to a given vibration, nay merely remain alert, or may dart from it, depending upon a variety of factors—such as familiarity with such vibrations, his own physiological activity at the time (whether seeking food, seeking a mate, spawning, spent or just resting), or outside factors of light, temperature and water content that may or may not influence his response to vibration. Just why a certain fish demonstrates active or passive behavior when hearing water vibrations is a proposition which demands individual investigation. It is not in itself a proof of hearing in the one case and failure to hear in the other, as might be supposed.

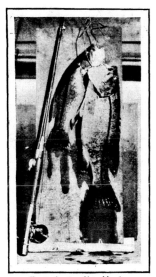

Showing location of lateral hearing lines in small-mouthed bass.

Another interesting fact was developed in the course of experimentation. Fish recover from a vibration which stimulates them and return to their normal activity very shortly after the vibrations cease. In fact, it seems clear that they arc disturbed by the vibrations only so long as- the vibrations continue—they seem to have little or no power to remember that they heard anything after the actual hearing ceases. This would lead to the conclusion that a fish, frightened by the footfall of an approaching angler, would be as easily caught when the vibrations ceased to reach it as it would have been before hearing the steps of the fisherman. And were it not for the fact that other factors enter into the equation, such as sight and change of location due to the run away from the vibration, this is probably true and would work out in everyday fishing practice. The half hour of rest that seems necessary after a fish has been driven from under an overhanging bank is, therefore, probably the result of factors other than the vibrations producing hearing.

In conclusion, then, we may safely say that fish hear and hear well, but that they cannot hear vibrations of the air—vibrations that are common sounds to you and to me; that fish respond to heard vibrations sometimes by flight from the source of the vibrations, sometimes by a greater degree of alertness, and sometimes by a positive reaction toward the source; that fish may change their reaction by becoming accustomed to certain regular water sounds; that failure to react is not a sign of failure to hear; and that their "memory" of sounds heard is almost, if not quite, as fleeting as the duration of the vibrations causing the- sounds. Shout if you wish, but have a care how you use your feet.

With Bait and Fly

Edited by SHERIDAN R. JONES

Life Histories of Live Baits

No. I—The Helgramite

Originally published in OUTER'S RECREATION, *January 1922*

GOGGLE goy, bell devil, flip-flap, bogart, alligator, crock, Ho Jack, clipper, crawler, snake-doctor, dragon, amly, conniption bug, hell-diver, water grampus, dobson or just plain helgramite—which? Surely there are not many of our stream insects that have as many vernacular names. And yet, perhaps, the term helgramite is the most universally used of all, especially among anglers. However, the fact that anglers generally are prone to call the larvae of many of the water insects by this name, has led us to present the life history of this most striking and curious creature. And we shall from time to time feature other live baits in the same way in order that the readers of this department may become more familiar with their habits.

It is a common thing among insects to have two active and independent stages during the course of their life histories. The first stage is the period of growth, and extends from the hatching of the egg until the time when the insect has reached a proper size for transformation into the adult or second stage. This latter stage is frequently of short duration and permits only of eating, the deposition of the eggs, and then death. In the larval stage the animal is usually a crawler, actively engaged in the pursuit of food and equipped with powerful jaws which it uses to advantage for both offense and defensive purposes. The adult is generally winged and emerges from a dormant stage (pupa) assumed by the larva preparatory to this change—an act known as transformation. Such an insect is the dobson.

The adult dobson is a large

Upper: The adult dobson in flight (female). Lower: The larval dobson, or helgramite

creature, frequently spreading more than four inches from tip to tip of wing. It possesses four wings as shown in the illustration where the insect is pictured in flight. When at rest, however, the wings are folded over the back, one upon the other, so as to present a narrow outline to the body and a flat upper surface, very similar to the winged ant and stonefly. The female and mate are similar in size and coloration (lead color) and in all respects save the mouth parts, which, in the female, are biting jaws, but in the male huge curved tusks fully an inch in length. These tusks cause one to fear the male more than the female, but, as a matter of fact, they are used only in holding the female at the mating time and do not function as jaws. One who has captured many of these creatures soon learns that here, as in many other phases of animal life, the female is "more deadly" than the male, as many a nipped finger will bear witness.

Some time in June the dobson is seen on the wing, flying about lights in the dusk of the evening or along the streamside. It is at this season that they are so frequently brought to one's attention by amateur scientists as "most remarkable and rare bug." Eggs are deposited upon most anything that overhangs the water, frequently the leaves of trees or rock ledges, in white masses about the size of a man's thumb nail and the larvae, on hatching, fall down into the water, where they seek shelter under the loose rocks. Here their life is spent in devouring other aquatic insect larvae, such as stoneflies and May-flies, and here they remain for nearly three years, feeding, growing, and furnishing food for black bass and other larva-feeding fish. At this stage they possess three pairs of well developed legs, biting mouth parts, and a pair of caudal tubercles, by the aid of which they cling to the rocks and other objects of the stream bed. Two rows of plamentous gills adorn the sides of the abdomen and help to give the creature a weird and dreadful appearance.

When ready for the final transformation, spiracles, characteristic of air- breathing insects, supplant the gills and the larva crawls out on the bank and seeks some hiding place under a stone, board, log or decaying branch, there to hollow out a cell and to pass into the pupa stage. This takes place usually in May and the transformation into the adult is accomplished in about thirty days. The pupa is a very pale yellow in marked contrast to the tough brown larva and the lead-colored adult, and is very soft and tender. All three stages of the dobson are valuable, but the toughness of the larva, its long life on the hook and its characteristic wiggle, make the larval stage the most suited to the needs of the bait angler.

The best helgramites for bait are those obtained directly from the bed of the stream before the development of the air functioning spiracles. When the larva once seeks the bank it becomes averse to water conditions and is less active on the hook and less tenacious of life. They may be obtained easily by wading out into the ripples and, holding a net on the down streamside, overturning the loose rocks. The bait will be swept down into the net by the force of the current. However, very acceptable larvae may be taken from under rocks and logs along the streamside, especially the rotting logs of some old mill dam. The hook should be inserted under the collar only, to insure long life and a plenteous wiggle, or the helgramite may be fastened to the hook by a bit of thread or a rubber band—method employed by many anglers with great success.

APPENDIX E: POPULAR FRESHWATER GAMEFISH

Edited by SHERIDAN R. JONES

The Fresh Water Angler

A series of chapters on modern fresh water angling wherein American inland waters, sport-giving fish, tackle and strategy are being considered in their relation to fishing as a means of recreation.

By Sheridan R. Jones

Originally published in OUTDOOR RECREATION, *December 1926*

THE large-mouthed black bass, *Micropterus salmoides*, is undoubtedly the most important member of the sunfish family, *Centrarchidae*, because of its abundance, its size in certain waters, and the further fact that it has made bait-casting history. The large-mouth is closely pressed by its smaller-mouthed cousin, *dolomieu*, for a leading role in the play of anglers but no one may safely say which bass plays the better part. Each fish has its supporters, even to the point of heated argument, but there is glory enough for all in the strike and in the fight of any bass. What matter if its mouth be large or small?

The natural habitat of the large-mouthed black bass was, originally, far more restricted than it is at the present time. Due to successful planting, dating from as far back as 1853 when the Potomac was stocked with fish crudely carried in the tender of a locomotive, the large mouth has been distributed widely and may now be found in suitable waters from Canada to Mexico, north and south, and from the Atlantic to the Pacific, east and west. The bass has also been introduced into Europe; such countries as France, Germany, England, and others, now having this American game-fish in more or less abundance.

The large-mouthed bass is a very hardy fish, enduring great extremes of temperature. In the shallow waters of the south, where summer temperatures are excessive and where the water temperature follows that of the air very closely, these fish seem to thrive practically as well as in the ice covered lakes of the north. As is true in the case of all gamefish, however, sudden changes in water temperature are very serious, especially changes from high to low. Rapid increases from low to high temperatures do not seem to be as fatal to the large-mouth as to some others, notably the rock bass, but all sudden changes are to be avoided when any attempt at planting is made.

There does not seem to be a marked optimum temperature in the case of large-mouthed bass and, for this reason, it is possible to give them a somewhat wider distribution than is possible in the case of such fish as the brook trout. Coupled with their ability to withstand unfavorable water conditions is their voracious and almost omnivorous feeding tendency. This makes their distribution among varied waters most easy and, were it not for the fact that bass cannot be artificially propagated, a constant supply in all waters would be assured. Black bass cannot be "stripped" and the eggs cared for in the customary hatchery, brooding ponds being necessary where the parent fish can spawn and care for the young along natural lines.

The large-mouthed black bass is a true sunfish in every way, differing but in body length and in the possession of a somewhat larger mouth than most species. The accompanying plate will give an idea of its lines and also the general appearance of the dark markings that adorn the sides of the younger fish. These dark blotches are often so run together that they form a dark lateral line that is very pronounced in fish up to a pound or so in weight. It is well to bear in mind at this point that this will always distinguish the large-mouth from the small-mouth whenever it is present; the dark markings of the latter fish tending toward the vertical bands common to so many members of the sunfish family.

Micropterus salmoides has been blessed with a multitude of common names, chief among which are the following: Straw, grass, slough, moss, green, bayou, marsh, lake, yellow, and Oswego bass, jumper, welshhman, chub, and trout. The most appropriate names, and those most universally used, are big-mouth and large-mouthed black bass. There seems to be an opinion, popular in some districts, that the Oswego bass is a different fish. As a matter of fact there are but two black bass—the large-mouth and the small-mouth—and all the other descriptive names are but local terms applied, many of them, because the bass in certain waters have a marked color tendency. The color of any fish is determined, within the limits of its pigmentation, by the environment from which it is taken and the large-mouth, rich in color pigments, shows a great variety of ground colors and dark patterns. Regardless of the color and the pattern, however, the large-mouthed black bass can always be distinguished by noting the following points:

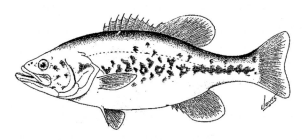

As was suggested previously, the young of this species have a black lateral fine, and this is often carried as a part of the pattern of quite mature fish. The scales on the cheek are large and there are ten or eleven rows to the seventeen or eighteen smaller scales on the cheek of the small-mouth. The mouth is exceptionally large for a member of the sunfish family, the maxillary (bony plate ending the upper jaw) reaching beyond the eye. Truly a big-mouthed bass! The general ground color is a silvery green, shading to a dark green or almost black back, and the three cheek stripes are dark and wholly without the bronze lustre of the small-mouth.

In size the large-mouth out-ranks the small-mouth by a considerable margin. The waters of the southland furnish an occasional fish of twenty pounds or better but fish of this size are by no means as common as popular opinion seems to indicate. In the northern districts a bass of seven or eight pounds is a big fish, while the average fish caught will run in the neighborhood of two or three pounds. I am fully aware of the fact that most bass excursions yield any number of five and six pounders, but we are speaking here of fish that have been weighed on tested scales, not fish "estimated" by reliable guides or guessed at by excited anglers. After a strenuous battle any fish looks large to the man who has cast the lure, but really big fish are not caught on every trip, at least not now-a-days.

As far as food is concerned the black-bass is an omnivorous feeder, demanding only that the morsel be alive or active. Minnows and the young of all fish, including their own offspring, frogs and salamanders, both mature and in the tadpole or pollywog stages, crayfish, adult and larval insect's, worms, these and other items make up the daily ration of the bass. At times the big-mouth will strike at anything that moves, birds, rodents, and snakes, as well as chips of bark, being not uncommonly found within their stomachs. We have been somewhat amused at discussions arising over the possible role of the frog in the daily ration of a bass, some claiming that they have never found a frog in the stomach of a bass. Most discussions of this nature arise from lack of experience or the desire of some to rush into print with "expert" opinions. We have not only found frogs in the stomachs of big-mouth bass on several occasions but we have fed small frogs to captive small-mouthed bass repeatedly. Digestion takes place rapidly in the stomach of a fish and frogs are difficult to catch unless the fish can work in very shallow water. There is little wonder that most bass do not contain frogs but rather minnows and crayfish, for these are everywhere abundant.

The greatest point of difference between the large and the small-mouthed black bass is, we believe, one of habitat. Prime conditions for the small-mouth are clear, cool water, rocks for hiding, and sand or gravel for spawning purposes. The large-mouth is a lover of the vegetation areas, both for a daily holding and for spawning purposes, while clear and cool waters are well liked but by no means as necessary as in the life of *dolomieu*. Vegetation choked lakes may often contain a supply of large-mouthed bass but the small-mouth will scarcely be found in waters of that type. There has been considerable discussion as to the relative fighting qualities of the two fish, based largely upon their differences in natural habitat, but we have failed to find marked inferiority on the part of either fish. We are sure that there is no bass that is a better fighter than the small-mouth of white-water streams; but a large-mouth taken from identical waters, as is often possible, is likewise a wonderful fish.

Though widely distributed and found in all parts of the country the big-mouth is always a big-mouth as far as habits and angling lore are concerned. Whether taken in Florida, Texas, California, or Wisconsin, Minnesota, Ohio, New York, or Tennessee, the large-mouthed black bass will be up to all of his customary tricks and wiles while the self same angling strategy will be required for his capture. The larger and heavier bass of the South will, as a rule, be more sluggish than their smaller northern brothers but the two, to five pound southern big-mouth will give as good an account of themselves as will any bass that is found in similar water and that is taken under similar conditions. One cannot expect a great struggle when taking bass from a warm and sluggish bayou; and this goes for northern fish as well as for those of the South.

We have previously stated that large-mouthed black bass are lovers of vegetation and cover. They are great fish to hide and to lie in wait for a passing bit of food. They strike promptly and without deliberation, when once they have decided to go into action, and this accounts for the fact that a bass will usually hit a lure from the side. Lily-pad areas are great hang-outs for big-mouth bass, while rushes, floating bog, deep-water weed-beds, and vegetation- bordered shore line-all furnish ideal spots in which to drop a lure.

The large-mouthed black bass spawns in the spring of the year, as do all members of the sunfish family, selecting a weedy spot in semi-shallow water where there is an abundance of bottom-growing vegetation. From the roots of these plants the male fans away the silt and prepares the nest for the females that are to come later into the spawning areas. Nest building occurs when the shallow waters have reached a temperature of from sixty to sixty-five degrees Fahrenheit. After the spawning has taken place the males continue to guard the nests and the newly hatched young until they are old enough to shift for themselves in the weeds of the shallow shoreline areas. Black bass have the parental instinct developed to a very high degree.

It is well to bear in mind the fact that bass continue spawning for a period of about two months, only a few eggs being developed at any one time. Our northern bass begin spawning about the middle of May and this runs their period of spawning over into the first weeks of July. There is very good reason, then, for the establishment of a late opening date on this, our most representative American game-fish.

| Kindly address all letters of inquiry to Mr. Jones or "Editor, Angling Department." It will help to avoid delay and bring a prompt response | With Bait and Fly | Your opinion on any angling subject may be of value to others. Let us have it for their benefit |

Edited by SHERIDAN R. JONES

The Fresh Water Angler

Chapter X—The Muskellonge

A series of chapters on modern fresh-water angling wherein American inland waters, sport giving fish, tackle and strategy are being considered in their relation to fishing as a means of recreation.

By Sheridan R. Jones

Originally published in OUTDOOR RECREATION, *July 1925*

OF all fresh water fish there is none that sends the red blood coursing through the angler's veins quite as does the mention of that charmed word 'lunge, for the muskellonge is, without question, the greatest game-fish of them all. No other proof of the above assertion is necessary than the mere fact that the taking of a fine specimen wins the life-long devotion of every angler to this giant member of the tribe of *Esox*. Once a 'lunge fisherman always a 'lunge fisherman is the rule and not the exception. The *raison d'etre* for the rule is more easily experienced than expressed. One cannot describe the taking of a muskellonge.

We have headed this chapter "Muskellonge." The spelling is but a personal reaction. The common name of *Esox masquinongy* is so wrapped up in the mysterious French-Indian folk lore that many spellings are considered equally correct, since all are but attempts to describe the musical syllables that fall from the lips of the native guide as the muskellonge makes his first dash for freedom. Someone has said that there are forty correct ways of spelling the name. We doubt if forty is sufficiently inclusive, but, for the benefit of those who may find interest in the possibilities of this word, we give a few. In the French we have *masque* meaning "mask" or "face," and *allongé* or *longé*, "lengthened" or "long." Thus, a long-faced fish. And some of the spellings are maskalonge, mascalonge, maskalunge, maskallonge, masquallonge, moskalonge, muscalonge, muskalonge, muskalinge, muskellunge, muskallunge, moskalonge, and many others. Often the real "Frenchy" masq'allongé and even nosconongé. Surely if one cares for the French twist there should be opportunity to make a satisfactory selection.

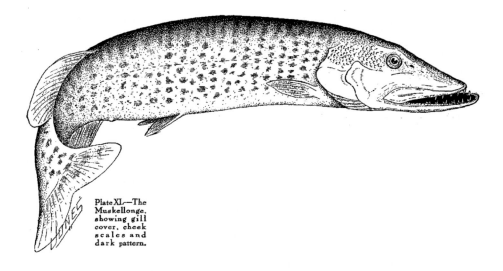

Plate XL—The Muskellonge, showing gill cover, cheek scales and dark pattern.

Again, from the Indian, we have *mas* meaning "great," *mask* meaning "ugly," and *kinonge, kenozha,* or *kinoje* meaning "pike"; while *kenose* is said to mean "long." Thus the fish may be a great pike, an ugly pike, or a great or ugly long fish. Certainly descriptive to say the least. Several of the Indian combinations are maskinonge (thus spelled in Canadian law), maskanonge, maskenonge, maskenozha, and maskinoje. And there are others!

We hesitate to suggest which of the several more commonly used spellings is best, for we do not know. Muskallunge and muskellunge are both very common in the more popular treatment of the sporting page, while in recent years there has seemed an increased leaning toward muskellonge—the spelling used in this chapter. In scientific writings we have noted that muskalonge is receiving "favorable mention"—so the reader may make his own selection with the full assurance that, as long as it sounds musky or masky, lungy or longy, nungy or nongy, it will pass muster and be accepted as meaning *Esox masquinongy*, the muskellonge.

The scientific term has had quite an experience as well. In some old English books we find this American pike styled *Esox estor*. According to other classifications the name is *Esox nobilior* quite commonly in use until the later and, we believe, the more approved Esox masquinongy put in its appearance. And so it stands today—Esox masquinongy, _the muskellonge.

The "musky," as this fish is dubbed in popular jargon, is strictly an American, and it seems that there were, originally, three races separated by more or less distinct geographic and habitat lines. Representatives of these three races are the St. Lawrence muskellonge, the Chautauqua or Ohio muskellonge, and the Northern, Wisconsin, or Unspotted muskellonge. Some hold to the opinion that these races are equivalent to species and that the scientific names should read *Esox masquinongy*, *Esox ohiensis* (possibly corrected to *ohioensis*), and *Esox immaculatus*, respectively. It is our own personal opinion, however, and that of some other ichthyologists, that these races are not worthy of more than *variety* standing. Taking the St. Lawrence race as an arbitrary type-form we should then have, in the order given, Esox *masquinongy masquinongy*, *Esox masquinongy ohioensis*, and *Esox masquinongy immaculatus*, a classification that is in line with the recently developed variations of the banded pickerel, *Esox americanus*, to which we shall call attention in our closing summary of the genus *Esox*. But the angler need not concern himself with scientific varieties. *Esox masquinongy* is sufficient and the varieties will be taken care of through the use of the more popular common names—St. Lawrence, Chautauqua, and Northern muskellonge.

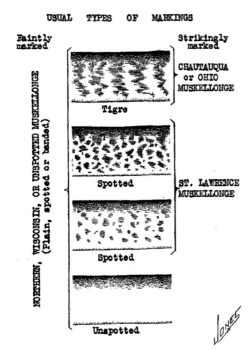

USUAL TYPES OF MARKINGS

Faintly marked

Strikingly marked

CHAUTAUQUA or OHIO MUSKELLONGE

Tigre

Spotted

ST. LAWRENCE MUSKELLONGE

Spotted

NORTHERN, WISCONSIN, OR UNSPOTTED MUSKELLONGE (Plain, spotted or banded.)

Unspotted

The plate accompanying this chapter gives a fairly good representation of the general characteristics of the muskellonge. A glance at the drawing and a comparison with the drawings of the great pike and the pickerel, used as illustrations in connection with a previous chapter, will show the same general pike lines with the exception that the muskellonge is very apt to be a bit heavier built in the region of the abdomen. This is not always the case however, for we have taken some very slim muskies and some "pot-bellied" great pike on occasion; but we find a greater number of the muskies running heavy in the region of the pelvic fin.

The drawing shows the one and only sure indication that the fish is a muskellonge— the cheek and opercle squammation. It will be noted that the lower half of both cheek and opercle (gill cover) are bare and scaleless, only the upper portions of each carrying the scales. This at once identifies our pike as a muskellonge, regardless of shape, fins, or color pattern. It is the one and unfailing mark upon which the angler may rely with full assurance. Such squammation indicates a muskellonge. To re-capitulate:

Upper half of cheek and gill cover scaled—muskellonge,

All of cheek and upper half of gill cover scaled—great pike,

All of cheek and all of gill cover scaled—pickerel.

Coming now to the matter of color pattern and the possibility of there being three species of muskellonge, or only one species with three varieties, we find ourselves, in the present day and generation, in a more or less tangled mass of detail due to the fact that these fish have been planted hither and yon until we are at a loss to draw any definite conclusions as to which fish is, and which is not, native to the district studied. From the information that is at hand, however, we may draw certain conclusions that may be of general interest.

The St. Lawrence muskellonge range seems to have been confined to that area of the North American continent from Lake Huron on toward the east and north, including portions of Ontario, Quebec, and northern New York—in fact, the drainage area of the St. Lawrence when this is considered in a large way. The maximum distribution, in point of area covered, matters little in a general account of this nature.

The Chautauqua muskellonge range lies to the south, from Chautauqua Lake on nearly to the Gulf, and passing through Ohio and neighboring states en route.

The Northern muskellonge range runs from considerably north of the Great Lakes around and through Minnesota and into Wisconsin. Thus one might start in Wis- consin, follow the Northern muskellonge up and around the Great Lakes, pass into the St. Lawrence muskellonge range to the east of Lake Huron, and on down into the Chautauqua; muskellonge range through western New York, Pennsylvania, and points southwest toward the Gulf.

But, as has been said, repeated plantings of muskellonge, especially in areas where the described ranges seem to have approached each other, have so mixed up the original distribution as to render it practically impossible to fix any fast rules as to the possible relationship existing between these three general types of fish. For this reason, while we shall give the general color pattern of the three suggested types as now understood, we shall also present what we consider a more satisfactory common terminology for the angler to employ in speaking of these fish, regardless of scientific relationship or the waters from which they may be taken. And, since the terms will be only those now in common use in muskellonge areas, we feel that the suggestion is timely and to the point. The St. Lawrence muskellonge is a spotted fish—dark spots upon a lighter ground color, a silvery gray. While there is considerable variation as to the size and the distribution of these spots, the fish may truthfully be styled as *strikingly marked* with dark spots.

The Chautauqua muskellonge is a banded fish—dark greenish cross bars on a rich brassy and metallic green, lighter ground color. Where the St. Lawrence fish is a silvery gray, the Chautauqua muskellonge is a brassy green; and the blackish dark pattern of the former is supplanted by a rich dark green. The St. Lawrence fish is of *drab* coloration; the Chautauquan is *brilliant*.

The Northern muskellonge runs from *banded*, through *short barred*, *spotted*, even to *spotless* in its color pattern—but the dark markings are *always less distinct*, somewhat blurred, and of a brownish hue. We have noted fish where the spots were rosy or margined with pinkish colors; seldom do they even approach the very dark spots of the St. Lawrence form, and the brilliant hues of the Chautauqua muskellonge are entirely wanting. If any metallic, sheen is present it is yellowish in lustre rather than green.

Plate XLI will give an idea of the usual types of markings found as a part of the color pattern of the several forms. The banded pattern is, almost universally, spoken of as "tigre muskellonge," the spotted and short barred as "spotted muskellonge" (or, if rather light and faint, as "star muskellonge"—a term carrying with it something of derision, though for no good and apparent reason), and the plain pattern as "unspotted muskellonge." It is the last mentioned fish that was given the name Great Northern Pike and Northern Pike, names which have been almost completely usurped by the great pike, *Esox lucius*, and which are quite commonly in use in the north country to designate a very large *lucius* form. It is to avoid confusion with the old application of the terms, Great Northern and Northern Pike, that it seems best to omit the "northern" from the common name of *lucius*, and to style him as the Great Pike.

Thus it comes about that the Northern muskellonge may be a "tigre musky," a "spotted musky," or an "unspotted musky"; the St. Lawrence muskellonge a "spotted musky"; and the Chautauqua or Ohio muskellonge a "tigre musky"—and a strikingly marked "tigre" at that! It is unnecessary for the angler to be more exact, for he cannot be absolutely sure of his fish because of the artificial distribution that has been made in recent years. Nor need he worry, for, spotted or unspotted, tigre or star, *Esox masquinongy* is a MUSKELLONGE!

APPENDIX F: SPECIALIZED GLOSSARY OF TERMS

ANIMAL DISTRIBUTION: The study of the habitats and locations of living species.

BAIT CASTING: A fishing method using medium to heavy tackle for large species of game fish such as Pike, Muskellunge, and Bass.

BIOLOGIST: A scientist who studies living things and their life processes.

CHASSIS: Supporting framework for the body of an automobile.

FISHING TACKLE: The equipment used to capture fish for sport. Includes rods, reels, lures, lines, sinkers, hooks, nets, etc.

FLY CASTING: A fishing method using specialized light weight tackle, designed to cast very light artificial baits, for nearly all species of game fish.

GENETICS: The branch of biology dealing with heredity and variation.

ICHTHYOLOGY: A branch of zoology dealing with fishes.

LURE: Artificial bait used to catch fish. Can be either hand-made or factory machined, and manufactured from almost any material.

MEMORABILIA: Items saved, collected, or preserved that are worthy of remembrance.

NATURALIST: One who studies animals and plants and holds that scientific laws account for everything in nature.

ORNAMENTAL TAXIDERMIST: An artisan who prepares the skin of animals, birds, and fish for preservation and mounting as permanent ornaments.

PLANT GEOGRAPHY: The study of the distribution of plants, trees and other growing organisms.

PLUG: *See Fishing Lure*.

REEL: A winch used to hold and retrieve line when fishing.

REPRODUCTION: To reproduce or bear offspring.

SPINNER: A kind of artificial fishing lure made primarily out of metal and designed to revolve a spinning blade around a wire body as a kind of fish attractor.

SPOON: A kind of artificial fishing lure made primarily out of metal, and usually with one treble or single hook.

TREATISE: An extensive written document on a subject.

TREBLE HOOK: A fishing hook with three barbs.

Appendix G: Time Line of Sheridan Jones' Life

1881   Born August 23, 1881.

1893   Preparatory School, University of South Dakota.

1902   Graduated with Bachelor of Arts Degree, University of South Dakota.

1906   Master of Arts & Science Degree, University of South Dakota.

1906   Teaching position, Baptist College, Grand Island, Nebraska.

       Married Miss Mae Freeman (died in 1926).

       Came to Iowa Falls, Iowa to teach at Ellsworth College.

1908-40 Biology Department Chair & Dean at Ellsworth Junior College, Iowa Falls, Iowa.

1910   Coached first basketball team for Ellsworth College, Iowa Falls, Iowa.

1914   Winning Article, *Outers Book*, Class "C" Bait Casting Tackle.

1916-18 Sabbatical leave for Graduate Study at the University of Michigan.

1918-29 Angling Editor of *Outer's Recreation* and *Outdoor Recreation Magazine*, formerly *Outer's Book*.

1924   *Black Bass and Bass Craft* book published by MacMillan Publishing.

1928   Married Vivian Klemme Ellis who had two sons, Donn and Klemme.

1936   Established Boat Club in Iowa Falls.

1956   Banquet at Ellsworth College to honor Professor Jones.

1958   Died at the age of 76 on April 12, 1958.

1958   Sheridan R. Jones Scholarship established to benefit biology students.

1961   Bullock - Jones Hall named in his honor at Ellsworth College.

BIBLIOGRAPHY

BOOKS

Carter, Arlan. *19th Century Fishing Lures: A Collector's Guide to U.S. Lures Manufactures Prior to 1901* (Paducah, KY: Collector Books, 2000).

Cavendish, Marshall. *America in the 20th Century, Vols. 1-13* (Tarrytown, NY: Marshall Cavendish, 2003).

Ciment, James, ed. *Encyclopedia of the Great Depression and the New Deal* (Armonk, NY: M.E. Sharpe, 2003).

Foggia, Lyla. *Reel Women: The World Of Women Who Fish* (Hillsboro, OR: Beyond Words, 1995).

Gallagher, Jack. *The Peppers of Rome* (Manning, SC: Gallagher, 1999).

Herd, Andrew. *The Fly: 2000 Years of Fly Fishing History* (UK: Medlar Press, 2005).

Hilyard, Graydon. *Carrie Stevens: Maker of Rangeley Favorite Trout and Salmon Flies* (Mechanicsburg, PA: Stackpole Books, 2000).

Johnson, Victor Sr. and Victor R. Johnson, Jr. *Fiberglass Fly Rods: The Evolution of the Modern Fly Rod from Bamboo to Graphite* (Boulder, CO: Centennial Publications, 1996).

Keane, Martin J. *Classic Rods and Rodmakers* (NY: Winchester Press, 1976).

Kelly, Mary Kefover. *The Origins of American Angling* (Cincinnati, OH: The Whitefish Press, 2008).

Larson, Todd E.A. *The History of the Fish Hook in America* (Cincinnati, OH: The Whitefish Press, 2007).

- - - - - - . *Pflueger Profiles: Essays on the History of Enterprise Manufacturing Company, Makers of Pflueger Fishing Tackle* (Cincinnati, OH: The Whitefish Press, 2006).

Luckey, Carl. *Old Fishing Lures & Tackle: Identification & Value Guide, 6th Edition* (Iola, WI: Krause Publications, 2007).

Marbury, Mary Orvis. *Favorite Flies and their Histories* (NY: Wellfleet, 1990).

Muma, John. *Old Flyrod Lures* (Belleville, IL: Great Lakes Initiatives, 2001).

Murphy, Dudley & Edmisten, Rick. *Fishing Lure Collectibles* (Paducah, KY: Collector Books, 2001).

Pfeiffer, C. Boyd. *Our Fishing Heritage: Tackle & Equipment.* (Minnetonka, MN: North American Fishing Club, 1999).

Roberts, Bill and Robbie Pavey. *The Heddon Legacy: A Century of Classic Lures* (Paducah, KY: Collector Books, 2002).

Ruby, Wayne. *The Pflueger Heritage: Lures & Reels 1881-1952* (Paducah, KY: Collector Books, 2008).

Smith, Harold. *Collector's Encyclopedia of Creek Chub Lures & Collectibles* (Paducah, KY: Collector Books, 2002).

Streater, Richard, et al. *The Fishing Lure Collector's Bible* (Paducah, KY: Collector Books, 1999).

Waterman, Charles F. *Fishing in America* (NY: Holt, Rinehart & Co., 1977).

White, Karl. *Fishing Tackle Antiques & Collectibles, Vols. 1-3* (Luther, OK: Holli Enterprises, 2002).

Vernon, Steven K. *Antique Fishing Reels: Your Illustrated Guide to Identifying and Understanding U.S. Patented Models Through 1920* (Mechanicsburg, PA: Stackpole Books, 1985).

WEB SITES

HISTORY & COLLECTIBLES

Clark's Classic Fly Rod Forum
http://clarksclassicflyrodforum.yuku.com/

Dr. Todd Larson's History of Fishing & Tackle
http://fishinghistory.blogspot.com/

Ellsworth Community College
http://www.iavalley.cc.ia.us/ecc/

The National Fishing Lure Collector's Club
http://NFLCC.org/

Sheridan R. Jones Web Site
http://sheridanrjones.com/

Steve Vernon's Antique Fishing Reels
http://antiquefishingreels.info/

Vintage Fishing Lures
http://Vintagefishinglure.com/

FISHING BOATS & MOTORS

Discover Boating
http://www.discoverboating.com/

Evinrude Motors
http://www.evinrude.com/

Lund Boats
http://lundboats.com/
Mercury Marine
http://MercuryMarine.com/

Pelican Sport, International
http://www.pelicansport.com/

Ranger Boats
http://www.rangerboats.com/

Tracker Boats
http://www.trackerboats.com/

Yamaha Motors
http://www.yamaha.com/

NEW YORK/CONSERVATION/FISHING

Adirondack Fishing Guide
http://www.fishadk.com/

Adirondack Life Magazine
http://adirondacklife.com/

N.Y. Dept. of Environmental Conservation
http://www.dec.ny.gov/

New York Game & Fish
http://NewYorkGameandFish.com/

1000 Islands Seaway Region
http://seawayregion.com/

FISHING/OUTDOORS/EQUIPMENT

Bass Pro Shops
http://www.basspro.com/

Cabela's
http://www.cabelas.com/

Lake Fishing
http://www.lake-fishing.com/

L.L. Bean
http://www.llbean.com/

Take Me Fishing
http://www.takemefishing.org/

FISH FINDERS

Furuno U.S.A.
http://www.furunousa.com/

Garmin
http://www.garmin.com/

Humminbird
http://www.humminbird.com/

Lowrance
http://www.lowrance.com/

TACKLE AND LURES

Abu Garcia
http://www.abu-garcia.com/

Berkley Fishing
http://www.berkley-fishing.com/

Daiwa U.S.A.
http://www.daiwa.com/

Eagle Claw
http://www.eagleclaw.com/site/

Jann's Netcraft
http://www.jannsnetcraft.com/

Laser Lures
http://www.laserlure.com/index.php

Live Target Lures
http://livetargetlures.com/

Mepps
http://www.mepps.com/

Orvis
http://www.orvis.com/

Panther Martin
http://www.panthermartin.com/

Pflueger
http://pfluegerfishing.com/

Plano Tackle Boxes
http://planomolding.com/

Rapala
http://www.rapala.com/

Ray Scott Outdoors
http://www.rayscott.net/

Shimano
http://fish.shimano.com/

St. Croix Rods
http://Stcroixrods.com/

X-Calibur
http://www.xcaliburtackle.com/

Zebco
http://www.zebco.com/

Z-Man Fishing
http://zmanfishing.com/

PERIODICALS/FISHING EXPERTS

Bassmaster Magazine
http://sports.espn.go.com/outdoors/bassmaster/

Bill Dance
http://www.billdanceoutdoors.com/

Field & Stream
http://www.fieldandstream.com/

The In-Fisherman
http://www.in-fisherman.com/

Outdoor Life
http://www.outdoorlife.com/

Sports Afield
http://www.sportsafield.com/site/index.php

Sport Fishing
http://www.sportfishingmag.com/

ABOUT THE AUTHOR

The year was 1957 in the late fall and Joe Hilko's 8th grade science teacher, Mrs. Armstrong, has announced a school-wide contest for the best science project. The contest winner would win a trip to summer conservation camp in Raybrook, New York. That day, Joe Hilko knew he was going to win this trip and immediately began to map out a plan to have the best project. Joe's winning project was "The Freshwater Gamefish of North America," and it was complete with essays and photos on all fish species including literature on fishing seasons, catch limits and laws, and the best places for angling in North America.

The conservation camp was all Joe expected and more: stream improvement work, fish propagation study, fish hatchery distribution, and of course, pond trout fishing. However, the best of all was Joe was chosen as one of a select few for an expedition to blaze a new trail across an Adirondack mountain. The log cabin dining hall and open air lean-to camping were highlighted by tales of the mountains such as "The Bearman" and "Escaped Prisoners" who have disappeared and have yet to be found. Joe's fabulous time at camp was soon dampened when he returned to learn about the required speech concerning his experiences at camp to be delivered to the Women's Club who sponsored him. After the speech the "ice was broken" and a shy kid from Schenectady, New York was destined to become a teacher and educator.

In 1965 Joe graduated from SUNY at Oswego and became a high school history teacher and soccer, basketball, and baseball coach. He attained an M.S. degree in Educational Communications at SUNY at Albany and became a tenured teacher and A-V Director at Delaware Academy in Delhi, New York. There were also six memorable years as copier sales supervisor with Pitney-Bowes, and in 1973 he became one of the top copier salesman in the nation.

Since 1980, Joe has been a publisher's representative in upstate New York consulting with many school and college libraries specializing in the latest social science reference books. He is also President of the Thermo-Bilt Company in Schenectady which makes the "Hilkoil" stainless steel water heating coils for the solid fuel stove appliance manufacturers in North America.

Joe and his wife Lynne have a new daughter Katelyn. Julie Ann and Mary Kay are daughters from his previous marriage. Lynne has been a major asset in the collection of the antique lures and the publication of this book, which represents one of the finest quality and historic antique fishing lure collections in North America. Most significant is the fact that the majority of these lures belonged to Sheridan R. Jones.

Joe and daughter Katelyn with several 20-inch Brown Trout caught in Lost Pond in New York's Eastern Adirondacks.

Individuals interested in contacting the author, preserving this museum quality lure collection, or have additional antique lures should write to Joe at:

Vintage Fishing Lures
P.O. Box 225
Ballston Spa, NY 12020
(1-800-244-9740)

Joe can also be reached via his web site at:

http://www.vintagefishinglure.com

and

http://www.sheridanjones.com

LURE INDEX

INDEX